PAGAN

From sex initiation, magic, moon-cult, tattooing, mutilation and other primitive rituals to family loyalty and solidarity

THEODOR REIK

 THE NOONDAY PRESS a division of
FARRAR, STRAUS AND COMPANY | NEW YORK

RITES IN JUDAISM

PROLOGUE

The studies in this book complement and continue the research into prehistoric Israel published in my tetralogy *Myth and Guilt, Mystery on the Mountain, The Creation of Woman* and *The Temptation*.

The reviews of those books were mostly negative, or at least reluctant. It was as if the reviewers were all giving the same opinion as one man:

> *This voice of the sluggard; I heard him complain,*
> *You have wak'd me too soon, I must slumber again.*

Yet I have received quite a few letters from attentive readers. There were scarcely any fan letters among them, but the writers thanked me for new insights gained from studying the books. It is possible that the essays in this volume will also awaken the interest of many readers. I feel that I must show my gratitude for the patience and the attention with which those earlier readers followed me on the tortuous and laborious ways I had to pursue in my research.

We Americans, when thanked, simply say "You are welcome." The French, so much more polite, say *"C'est moi qui vous remercie."*

Theodor Reik
New York, October 1963

CONTENTS

ONE

A HOME AWAY FROM HOME

1 | Introduction

It was my grandfather who first initiated me into the knowledge of Jewish rites—more will be said about him later—and who showed me a sukkah in a Vienna street, near a synagogue. I was perhaps eight years old then, and I still vividly remember my astonishment at the strange sight. There was a booth or kind of rustic cabin, covered with leafy branches and twigs instead of a roof. I remember that I wanted to look inside the booth, but Grandfather forbade me to enter; I understood only later that I was then too young to go into the booth.

The sukkah, seemingly so unique, fits well into the frame of other religious ceremonials. We need only think of the elaborate preparations made in Western civilization for religious festivals. They would greatly astonish not only a small boy but also a person educated in another culture. How strange it is to cut a fir tree, transport it into your house and erect it before Christmas, hang fruits and gifts on its branches, and decorate it richly! A tree belongs to the forest, does it not, not the home? Its transportation amounts literally to transplantation.

Or take an instance from Hebrew religion, the Feast of Booths (Sukkoth) in autumn. Observing the preparation for this festival, the casual witness will see that people have built a cabin or a hut outside the house. Moreover, they have roofed it with palm leaves and put all sorts of branches and fruits on and around it. Here are booths outside the house—booths standing, for instance, in the middle of Manhattan, covered with plants and leaves! It is as though the forest had penetrated the city. Why a booth if there is a house?

(An Australian aborigine watching these preparations would be amazed, but at the same time would notice something familiar in them: They would remind him somehow of customs in his native village.)

Someone who asks the meaning of both festivals will be told that they have a historical character. They are reminders of the greatest events in the history of two religions.

Christmas is the yearly celebration of the birth of Christ. The tree in the house is the Tree of Paradise reopened, the miracle-tree that bears flowers in the middle of the winter. The Israelites, asked the meaning of the booths, perhaps explain that they should remind us of the tents in which their ancestors dwelt when they wandered through the desert from Egypt to Palestine.

The experts, however, will inform the inquirer that historical explanations are late ones and that the origins of the festivals must be sought in the world of paganism. Most of the Christmas customs are not originally Christian, but heathen customs absorbed by the Church. The cradle of Christ, for instance, is borrowed from the cult of Adonis; the Yule customs come from the concepts of the *wilde Jagd* of the Teutonic god Odin; and so on. According to some scholars, the Feast of Booths originated in the worship of Adonis or from the ritual drama of the Canaanites—whose autumn festival included a banquet of the gods and the erection of a pavilion for them.

In this particular piece of research I am seeking to fathom the later layers of development in the story of the Feast of Booths and to discover its prototype in the prehistory of the Semites. I hope this can be accomplished with the help of the psychoanalytic method, which is used here as a research instrument that enables us to reach the concealed origin of individual and collective phenomena and to discover the decisive primal behind the recent.

It is plain that the Feast of Booths, as celebrated today by religious Israelites, is a relatively late derivative of an ancient custom. We are curious to discover what its prototype is, but much more we wish to learn what the prehistoric meaning of the feast was. The nature of this research is necessarily similar to that of a reconstruction by an archeologist who draws an outline of a prehistoric sanctuary, basing his attempt on the remnants of columns and stones. There is, of course, no guarantee that his reconstruction is correct; no one will ever again see the prehistoric building.

My attempt at reconstruction here is therefore not only venturesome and bold, but it also reaches beyond the unseen into the domain of the invisible. It recalls a story Jean Cocteau once told about one of his young nieces. Her parents had told her that an angel had brought her a brother. "Do you want to see your brother?" she was asked. "No," she said. "I want to see the angel."

We are like Cocteau's niece. We too want to see the angels,

but we know that is impossible. We shall be content if we can feel the movement of their wings.

11 | The setting of the feast

No wonder an Australian native would be reminded of tribal ceremonies when he watched the Feast of Booths. Features of the celebration are clearly primitive and magical; there were such rites in the time of the Temple of Jerusalem, rites of which only certain features survive today.

There was, for instance, the ceremony of water libation to induce rainfall. We know that similar rituals, based on sympathetic magic, were observed in many parts of the primitive world—for instance among the Mara tribe of northern Australia. In time of drought the tribal magician sprinkled himself with water and poured drops of it on the ground, believing that in this manner rainfall would be produced.[1] There is not much difference between this ceremony and one reported in the Mishnah—that a golden flagon filled with water was carried to the Temple in Jerusalem where the priest poured water upon the altar.

Another ceremony recorded in the Mishnah is also undoubtedly magical. On the evening of the first day of the Feast, men lit candelabra in the Court of the Women at the Temple, then danced in front of them and waved burning torches. Levites holding trumpets ascended the steps and, turning their faces westward, sounded prolonged blasts. They cried out: "Our forefathers, when they were in this place, turned their backs to the Temple of the Lord and their faces toward the rising sun in the East, but as for us, our eyes are turned toward the Lord."

These words leave no doubt that this ceremony was originally a magical one to rekindle and salute the rising sun.

There are many analogous rituals among primitive tribes and the people of antiquity, ceremonies the purpose of which was to cause the sun to rise.

But what about the center of the stage, that hut away from the house? There might be a faint reminder of something resembling such an arrangement in New Guinea or central Australia, but our Australian bushman cannot for the moment remember what it is.

We are beginning to focus our attention on this setting of the dramatic action.

It will help, perhaps, to comment briefly here about the dramatic character of ritual in general. Most modern investigators agree that drama and ritual were originally dramatic performances, "things done," as Jane Harrison calls them. Mowinckel [2] points out that rituals at the primitive level are procedures that bring about results by means of imitative actions (mimes, dances, processions, symbolic plays, and the like). These presentations are actions that aim to accomplish, for instance, the provision of food, rain, and sunshine.

If cult and ritual are thus originally dramatic plays ("All the world's a stage . . ."), what is the scene of the action, the setting? The answer to this question is particularly relevant since the setting not only functions as background for the action but also as a means of dramatic expression. We see before us a booth—the sukkah—that has, according to the Mishnah, at least three sides. It is not roofed except with lightly strewn leaves. It must not be lower than five feet or higher than thirty. And it must not be a permanent structure, since its erection is part of the commandment.

All adult males must eat and sleep in the booth; only women and children are exempt. The sukkah is not a comfortable dwelling place because it is exposed to the elements; rainwater, for example, may be baled out only under certain conditions. The Israelites who dwell in the booths must tolerate assorted hardships.

The booth is covered with branches and sometimes with fruit. The impression of a hut in the middle of the forest is intensified when the worshipers also carry a branch and a bunch of fruit. This they do, obeying the Biblical commandment "ye shall take you on the first day the fruit of goodly trees, branches of palm trees, and boughs of thick trees, and willows of the brook, and ye shall rejoice before the Lord your God seven days" (Lev. 23:40).

There are good analogies to such carrying of festive bunches of fruit. (Since we are concentrating here on the setting of the action, we shall not consider the symbolic significance of the citron [*ethrog*], the myrtle, the willow, and the bunch of fruit [called *lulah*] which the pious carry. We must also pass over the question of the significance of another rite called "beating Hosannas"—on the seventh day of the feast the faithful beat leaves off extra twigs upon the lectern while they recite the Hosanna litanies.)

Here, one might ask whether we are justified in considering the ritual of the booth the center of the festival. It will be necessary to discuss this question along with the significance of the whole feast. The Feast of Ingathering, as it is also called, was the final stage of a longer festive season whose parts are now represented by New Year, the Day of Atonement, and this Feast of Booths. The importance once attributed to the concluding feast is demonstrated by the fact that it was also known under the inclusive name The Festival.

What are the principal features of the celebration? Theodor Gaster enumerates three: the reaping of crops and fruits and the bringing in of the vintage, the performance of ceremonies for inducing rainfall, and the custom of dwelling in booths.[3] Gaster adds: "Of these usages the most important was the last, and it was this that gave the feast its popular name." Other scholars likewise consider the dwelling in the sukkah "the main feature" [4] or the "chief characteristic" [5] of the festival.

With confirmation of the opinion that dwelling in the tabernacle is the most important part of the festival, let us now survey the attempts to explain this characteristic feature. Such a survey will give us useful insights into the views of earlier researches concerning the meaning of the festival. Not content, like Ruth in the Bible story, with "gathering after the reapers," we are rather searching for a new field whose harvest is yet ungleaned.

III | Attempts at explanation

Here is a summary of the main interpretations of the Festival of Tabernacles and its meaning. Neither complete nor detailed, this survey only shows what the traditional and modern views of this feast's significance have been.

The most widely held opinion is that the Feast of Booths was originally a harvest festival. It has been pointed out that the booths were originally the walled cabins in which the harvesters lodged during the season—such cabins are still found in Palestine when reaping is in progress. This is the agricultural aspect of the feast observed by orthodox and conservative Jews for nine days and by reformed Jews for eight. We do not know in which month the Jews first celebrated the feast, but it is certain that it was a merry time, including song and dance, sometimes exceeding the limits of revelry. The prophet Amos, who visited the Temple at Beth-El during the autumnal festival, condemned it (Amos 5:2-20), and Isaiah said that even priests and prophets were drunk in the sanctuary (Isa. 38:7-8).

It is easy to criticize the theory that the feast is nothing but the successor of the old Canaanite autumnal festival marking the completion of harvest—even if one admits that it was only later so interpreted. We know nothing about the ancient festival before Ezra.

The decisive question here, as formulated by Hayim Schauss, is how did the sukkah develop from an ordinary shack at the time of the harvest into the central theme of a religious festival? How did such an important Jewish custom evolve from the natural practice of dwelling in a booth? Schauss correctly argues that building a shack and living in it during the harvest time was an ordinary occurrence.[6] Why then did it become a rule to erect such a booth during the festival?

I have taken this one view of that theory to represent many others and now turn to the traditional conception of the Feast of Booths. This attributes a historical significance to the feast and places its origin before the ancestors of Israel arrived in Canaan. According to this view, booths represent the tents in which the Hebrew tribes sheltered while they wandered through the desert from Egypt to the land God had promised them. Thus conceived, the Feast of Booths is the "logical sequel to Passover and Pentecost which commemorated the escape from bondage and the conclusion of the Covenant at Sinai." [7] It should not merely remind successive Jewish generations of the past, but, so to speak, cause them to share it.

Theodor Gaster justifiably calls this view fanciful, pointing to the cold fact that tents are not booths and that wood and green leaves are rarely available in deserts. He adds that through the ages Jewish scholars and teachers have felt "a little uneasy" about the story of the booths in the wilderness. Hayim Schauss, in his *Jewish Festivals,* calls the interpretation in the Pentateuch "forced" and "evolved in later times." [8] He adds that if the sukkah was really connected with the Exodus, then Pessach would be the appropriate time for dwelling in booths. He too points out that there is considerable difference between a tent and a booth. The tent of the desert Bedouins consists of a sheet of goatskin hung over poles driven into the earth, while the main feature of a sukkah is the open roof, covered with branches and leaves. Some of the rabbis of Talmudic times asserted that the sukkoth of the desert were not booths but were "clouds of glory," basing this interpretation on Isaiah (4:5-6).[9]

This is perhaps the appropriate place to mention some interpretations tracing the origin of the Feast of Booths farther back than the entrance into Canaan. Of these theories, I have chosen the suggestion of Theodor Gaster in his characterization of the feast. In his scholarly *Thespis*, Gaster writes that we know many of the rites of that festival "only in their mythical transmutation." [10] He recognizes, however, traces of the original mimetic performances, for instance in the combat between the god and the dragon (or some similar adversary) referred to in Old Testament psalms, and also in the installation of the god in a special pavilion. He sees in Zachariah 14:16 a reference to the triumphant reaffirmation of the god's sovereignty since in this passage the Feast of Booths is connected with a pilgrimage to Jerusalem and the worship of the "King Jaweh Sebaot." He thus traces the feast back to the Babylonian myth of Marduk, who was installed in a pavilion after he had defeated the dragon Tiamat. In a Canaanite text a custom is mentioned of booths being constructed at a seven-day festival. Gaster suggests that the booths originated in these pavilions erected for various deities.

Even if we admitted that there is some justified core to this interpretation and could see adaptations in the rites of the Babylonians and Canaanites, we would still be puzzled about the original meaning of the booths and of the festival.

Only a few references are necessary to characterize the modern "symbolical" interpretation of the booths as they appear, for instance in the sermons and addresses of contemporary rabbis.[11] Rabbi Abraham N. Rutnick said that the tabernacle also teaches us that the Jews have not always been accorded freedom "to enjoy their culture and civilization in environments of peace, security and justice." Rabbi Mowshowitz wrote that the Sukkoth festival should remind us "that the most permanent, the most lasting kind of building is the one fashioned out of noble visions and more creative lives," while Rabbi Mordecai Kirshblum said that the festival "symbolizes man's dedication to the noble principles of freedom, learning and religious truth."

From the vast literature on the subject I would like to consider only a few papers that stand, so to speak, on the fringes of the pertinent treatises and books. The first, by A. J. Wensinck, compares the Feast of Booths with the Arabic New Year.[12] Robertson Smith had already tentatively connected the custom of dwelling in tabernacles with the taboo of the house. Wensinck mentions the traditional explanation that sees in the custom a continuation of people dwelling in booths during the harvest time. He says "I must confess that the nearly universal belief in this explanation is somewhat startling to me." [13] Since this wine-harvest custom is never mentioned in the Old Testament, the current explanation seems a priori inadequate. He also rejects the theory that traces the tabernacles back to the tents of the Exodus and calls the booths "real *Laubhuetten*."

Wensinck also points out that in certain critical periods, the belief in the taboo of the house is also found in the Arab world. The meaning becomes clear when one recognizes that "the house as well as places provided with a roof were to be avoided." During the seven days of the feast the booths have taken the place of the house that is considered dangerous. He refers to a passage in the old book of Bodenschatz (II, 237), which states that the Jews "when they have to go out of their tabernacles, are very shy and they do not want to be seen."

The student of the rites will agree that Wensinck is justified in emphasizing that the most significant feature is the fact that the booth is a tabernacle away from the house. It must be significant that the males must dwell in the booths during the festival and avoid the house. He has a point there, but only a point—and this is too small a mark to build a theory on. He misses other points.

I shall finish this survey with the most recent interpretation of the rites that has come to my knowledge, the hypothesis that Hans Joachim Kraus published in 1954.[14] Kraus takes his point of departure from J. Wellhausen's concept of *Denaturierung der Feste*.[15] Feasts that were originally Canaanite became "denaturalized" and were transformed. Kraus refers to a paper by A. Alt in which Alt remarks that the historical interpretation of the festival (Lev. 23:42) contains an "anachronism" since the Hebrew tribes, led by Moses, lived in tents and not in booths.[16] Kraus poses the interesting question: "Is it not possible that behind that anachronism is a cultic reality?" [17] This would mean that the Israelites originally celebrated the festival in memory of their dwelling in tents and later assimilated the custom of the Canaanites and spent the week in booths.

In searching for a prephase of a tent festival Kraus finds a trace of the existence of an early feast in the old tradition of Exodus (33:7-11): "And Moses took the tabernacle, and pitched it without the camp, afar off from the camp, and called it the Tabernacle of the congregation. And it came to pass, that every one which sought the Lord went out unto the tabernacle of the congregation, which was without the camp. And it came to pass, when Moses went out unto the tabernacle, that all the people rose up, and stood every man at his tent door, and looked after Moses, until he was gone into the tabernacle. And it came to pass, as Moses entered into the tabernacle, the cloudy pillar descended, and stood at the door of the tabernacle, and the Lord talked with Moses. And all the people saw the cloudy pillar stand at the tabernacle door: and all the people rose up and worshiped, every man in his tent door. And the Lord spake unto Moses face to face, as a man speaketh unto his friend. And he turned again into the camp. . . ."

One must acknowledge the courage with which Kraus refuses what he calls all *Pauschaltheorieen* (lump theories) that try to explain the Festival of Booths in a simplified manner. We must also grant that his attempt to reach the primal or original type of the festival is in principle correct. It is necessary to search for this primal type in the prehistoric past and to find it beneath the tradition and the later transmutations. The question remains whether this theory goes far enough back—and if one has not to turn to even earlier and more primitive phases of evolution to reach that primal period of the booth.

We have now presented a short survey of the theories on the festival. I could say "The choice is yours," but I shall now present my own theory.

IV | A new approach

This venture would never have been undertaken and pursued if I had approached the problem in the spirit of theoretical speculation and if I had explored it with traditional methods. The advantage I enjoyed, compared with previous explorers, was that I could use the psychoanalytic method of research that has not yet been applied in the investigation of this and similar problems. The inquiring mind, provided with a new instrument of search, will be able to recognize connections and associations of ideas that have been neglected or missed by previous investigators.

A certain moral courage in viewing and pursuing these newly recognized connections is certainly requisite for such a daring voyage of discovery. We venture it in the spirit of *"Toujours de l'audace!"* [18]

To clear the deck, we must dismiss previous attempts at interpretation: the theories concerning the reminder of tents during the Exodus, the Canaanite cabins during the harvest, and so on. Some of those interpretations certainly have merit, but they refer to late adaptations of the original customs. Our present voyage will lead us farther off and into a phase of prehistory even more remote. The point of departure is the impression of the setting of the Feast. Why do we choose the setting and not the ritual of the Festival of Booths itself; why not the ceremonies of water libation or the beating of branches and other rituals? There are good reasons. The rituals and ceremonials are subjected to more major changes than the scene, which remains relatively the same. Furthermore, all students of the festival agree that living in the booths is the most significant feature of the feast; we are therefore justified in turning special attention toward the dwelling place during the week of celebration.

There is finally the very setting, the scene in which the ritual actions take place. A criminal trial is, as Jerome Michael of the Columbia Law School once characterized it, "a play without a playwright." (Only Fundamentalists believe that the Lord was the playwright!) If this characterization is correct, the setting of the play deserves to be considered first, since it is what meets the eye when the curtain rises. In this particular case, the setting is especially worthy of attention because it remains the same for the whole play, for the whole time the festival is celebrated.

What do we see when the curtain goes up? There is a booth or, if you wish, a large hut remote from the house. This booth has no roof and is covered with and surrounded by leaves and branches. What does this mean? What impression does the booth, this hut away from the house, convey? As the central part of the setting it is certainly primitive enough, as simple and plain in style as most parts of the scene in our theaters. In some of the plays we attend these days, we see pieces of carton and other simple material that—painted and cut in an appropriate manner—represent the furniture of a room, the trees of a forest or of a park, and so on. The illusion produced by the set is willingly accepted by us; we feel transported into a dining room or into a park. (Here is a temporary "suspension of disbelief.")

In the same spirit we are looking at the sukkah, the booth surrounded by leaves and branches. The impression it evokes and which is doubtless intended is of a hut or house in the forest. The objection could be raised here, of course, that the booth is only at a modest distance from the lodging or, in modern times, from the synagogue. There is, for instance, a sukkah erected in the yard of the Jewish Theological Seminary in New York only a few steps from the lecture rooms and the library—in the heart of Manhattan. This same objection could be made to the location and the character of the various settings in our theaters. We are not present in a park or in a church when we, the audience, look at the scene of a play; we are in a small building in one of New York's side streets where there is no park or church. We succumb to a voluntary illusion here, as we do in viewing the booth.

I am going beyond the basic point. The erection of the tabernacle not far away from the house is perhaps an adaptation of a later phase; in the prehistoric time in which we are searching for the primal type of the feast, possibly the booth was really in the forest and far away from the houses of the village. The illusion intended and created by the surrounding palm leaves and branches thus reflects an actual state as it once existed in the original form of the festival. The distance of the booth or hut from the village was then considerable and shrank only much later as a manifestation of cultural change, as a result of religious transmutation.

If we tentatively accept the suggestion, we arrive at this view of the origin of the festival: There was once a large hut in the forest, far from the usual dwelling places of the Hebrew tribes. In this booth the males of the tribes lived for a specific period. The place was not accessible to women or to boys who had not yet arrived at a certain age.

Did we not in imagination introduce an Australian aborigine as an observer of the ritual of the tabernacle feast, and did it not remind him somehow of tribal customs? If he now sees the booth covered with palm-branches, it would bring to his mind a familiar hut destined only for men. He is reminded of the *Männerhaus* or of the hut in which the young boys spend many months before they are circumcised and in which they are taught the tribal rites. Perhaps the sight of the booth persistently reminds him of the primitive structure in Australia where the secret societies are housed.

An abundance of apparently insurmountable objections and contrary reasons will, of course, be provoked by the suggestion of connecting the tabernacle of the Feast with the *Männerhaus* or the puberty-huts of Australian and Melanesian tribes. Is it not fanciful; is it not even fantastic and bizarre to search for a resemblance between the tabernacle of Hebrew tribes in Palestine and those huts in a remote continent? What have these temporary booths of a religious festival to do with the customs of native tribes, some of which are still in the Stone Age?

Yet we have not claimed that there is an identity of customs or purposes between those two buildings. We recorded only the possible thought-association of an Australian aborigine observing the sukkah. The primitiveness of the setting does not disturb him, nor does the nearness of houses divert him. The palm-covered booth brings those houses of men at home to his mind. Our task is now to find out whether there is any possible actual connection between the two.

The argument that the customs of the prehistoric Hebrew tribes cannot be compared with those of extremely primitive Australian aborigines can easily be rebutted. We need only point out that some eminent scholars were keen in recognizing the model of the sukkah in the huts of pagan Canaanites or in the pavilion reserved for Marduk or Adonis of the Babylonians. They did not shy away from searching for the primal type of the tabernacle in the more ancient cultures of the Egyptians or the Accadians. It is only that we went beyond the theories of those Orientalists and historians in our backward look. We arrived at an even older and more primitive phase of evolution when we suggested that there may be a connection between the tabernacle of the Hebrew tribes and the forest huts of Australian aborigines.

Far from asserting that the *Männerhaus* and the booth are identical, we ventured to suggest that there is a distant resemblance. This resemblance can best be compared to the one that exists between an ancestor and his great-grandchild. Since this exploration has a genealogical purpose, our study is justified in digging up such resemblances and in noting them.

The theoretical and creative justification of comparisons of this kind is amply shown by the research work of such prominent scholars as W. Robertson Smith, James G. Frazer, Mircea Eliade, and others. To quote only one of them, Frazer, who applied the comparative method to the myths and stories of the Old Testament, states that the ancient Hebrews also had an early phase of savagery and that many traces of the old customs and ideas survived in their rites and institutions long after they had reached higher levels of civilization. The comparative method "applied to the ancient Israel allows us to pierce the dead wall which, till lately, appeared to block the path of the inquirer." [19]

In our study we shall combine this comparative method with that of psychoanalysis, which tries to penetrate the early unknown history of individuals as well as of groups and people. Psychoanalytic theory asserts that the repressed in the history and prehistory of a people is really immortal and indelible. It will make itself felt in the descendants of the disavowed and denied past—in institutions and in customs that seem to originate in later strata of history. The enquirer, endowed with this new research tool, will find clues to the ideas of those vanished generations, and this scholarly detective will through patient interpretation finally arrive at the reconstruction of that surviving prehistoric past.

So much (perhaps too much) for the justification of the comparison between the tabernacle of the ancient Hebrew tribes with the huts of savage and barbarous Australian and African peoples.

v | Reconstruction

We have seen that some scholars trace the custom of the booth back to the Canaanites, and a few even to the earlier rites of Babylonians or Egyptians. I believe that this search for the origin of the Feast of Tabernacles was broken off prematurely and that we must return to prehistoric times to discover its original home. We must reach farther back, into a haze of unremembered past.

It is now nearly universally assumed that the Semitic tribes from which the ancient Hebrews much later emerged and formed a separate people lived at first in Arabia. At the dawn of history those Semites who had once inhabited the rich tropical lands of the Sahara and the great Arabian coun-

tries gradually migrated westward. The recession of the
last icecap made those once-so-fertile regions arid and
changed them into deserts. From all these areas there was a
gradual "migration of animals and their parasite man" as a
recent book calls it,[20] until the life of both concentrated in
the valleys and marshes of the Euphrates, the Tigris, and the
Nile.

As the youngest of the migrants, Aramean and kindred
people turned in the same direction. Among them were then
—at the beginning of the thirteenth century B.C.—the tribes
from which the Hebrews emerged after having been mixed
with other people.

The origin of that hut in the forest, of the booth which is
the prototype of the Hebrew tabernacle, is to my way of
thinking here, in the original Arabic home of the Semitic
tribes. If this idea is correct, the notion of a pavilion for a
god or even of the Canaanite hut at harvest time could be
easily explained as derivatives of that primal tabernacle. The
sukkah calls up the picture of a hut from a tropical region
full of palms. The scholars who discover the origin of the
Tabernacle Festival in Babylon or Canaan jubilantly bark up
the wrong tree—from which the branches and leaves for
the booth are taken.

Said another way, the primal type of the booth or hut for
the Hebrew feasts is a building somewhere akin to the *Männerhaus* or the dwelling place of boys at puberty. This primitive residence was once erected in the forests of Arabia.

The Semitic tribes of the Neolithic age in Arabia were not
too remote in their customs and ideas from the Australian
and African aborigines. They must have shared with them
certain notions or survivals of rites and customs as we find
them in the savage tribes even today. I consider the custom
of the booths, the whole festival—of course, very much
changed in its character and in many details—a surviving
remnant of rituals performed by long-vanished generations.

At this point the comparison of the sukkah with the *Männerhaus* sets in. It is a long shot, but it is possible, if one accepts the psychoanalytic assumption that memory traces of the prehistoric past survive in later generations. The Men's House is originally the dwelling-place of bachelors, but its function was enlarged with the emergence and evolution of the institution of *Männerbünde* (clubs) and secret societies. The hut was once the dwelling place of pubescent boys who were instructed there in the secret tribal rituals.

As Mircea Eliade points out in his recent book, the initiation cabin symbolizes the maternal womb.[21] The whole initiation ceremonial has the significance of death and resurrection. "The Mystery begins everywhere with the separation from the family, especially from the women and a 'retreat' into the forest." The boy who is carried into the forest at night is mourned by his family and his clan as though he had died. The forest thus symbolizes the beyond.

After the ceremonies held at the attainment of puberty, there are others, those of the secret societies or men's societies. These mysteries, reserved for adults, have the same symbolic ritual of death and resurrection as does the initiation of boys. To Eliade and to many other students of comparative religion the conclusion is "irresistible that the men's secret societies, the *Männerbünde,* derive from the mysteries of tribal initiations." [22]

If the Men's House was originally a place lived in during initiation ceremonies, its late forms are those of the temple. The tribal sanctuaries are derivatives of the typical Men's House.[23]

It is, of course, impossible to say at what period the booth or sukkah replaced the cabin of initiation—to fix a date for the period when and how the tabernacle became the most conspicuous survival of the Men's House. We are not now considering the temple or the congregation or the *schul* of Eastern Jewry because they belong to later times. We may assume that the transition must have taken place long after the Hebrew tribes became a confederacy, but even this is not certain.

The causes of later changes are much easier to guess. They are mostly of the nature of adaptation to the civilizations or religious rites of the people in whose midst the Hebrews lived. Yet there are other transformations determined by Yahwism and by the great reforms enforced by Moses. When the Hebrew tribes became a "people of priests, a whole nation," the original secret society of the tribes was extended to encompass all males from a specified age on. The Men's House was replaced by the temple.

In regard to the booths in which the men at first spent many weeks, some changes were induced rather late by several factors. Theodor Gaster concedes that of the seasonal festivals of the Jewish year the Feast of Tabernacles has suffered most from the conditions of modern life and that "for all the tenacity of its observance it is the one which possesses for the modern Jew the least contemporary relevance." [24] Gaster enumerates a number of reasons for this change, mostly of a practical kind. Previously the sukkah was erected near one's home. In modern times the booths became communal and were built in the courtyard of the synagogue. Strictly speaking, this development is really a regression to the older form. If my thesis that the tabernacle is the survival of the primitive Men's House is correct, we recognize that there was only one such hut for the tribe.

More radical is the fact that the booth is moved into the vicinity of the house, while the Men's House of primitive tribes—according to the reports of all anthropologists and missionaries—is in the woods or in the jungle. We know that the setting of the sukkah tries to evoke the sense that this house is still in the middle of the forest, very far off from other houses.

Life in the Men's Houses was hard, especially for the boys

at puberty. The roofless sukkah, the successor of the primitive dwelling place, was similarly once not a comfortable place to sleep and eat in. But doing so was a strict religious obligation. The modern amelioration of the custom requires that at least one meal must be taken in the booth each day during the week. A social function has taken the place of the old custom and the sukkah is, in Gaster's words, "reduced to an artistic showpiece." [25]

In spite of all the transformations, the ancient and primitive element in the tabernacle customs is still recognizable. There are even certain rites that can be traced back to the puberty rites of savage tribes. There is, for instance, the rite of "beating Hosannas," in which extra twigs are beaten. Gaster reminds us of ancient Greek rituals in which human scapegoats were beaten with squills of willows to ensure fecundity. I would rather refer to the many ordeals which the boys of primitive tribes have to undergo during their long initiation celebration.

There is the passage from the prophets (Ez. 38:18-39:16) chosen to be read on the Sabbath. It deals with the war the Lord will wage against Gog and Magog at the end of days. What has this belligerent prediction to do with the Festival of Tabernacles? It seems entirely in the wrong place. Even Gaster thinks "it is difficult to see why the latter passage should have been selected, for it would seem to have no sensible bearing upon the Feast of Booths." [26] I am unwilling to accept Gaster's explanation. I would rather again refer to the puberty rites, at the conclusion of which the boys went out to fight hostile tribes. The fathers encouraged the young men to kill many enemies. Those passages are an echo of such combative and belligerent phrases.

Finally, I would like to mention a single, representative case that proves that an old and forgotten notion returns from the area of the repressed and bursts into the religious atmosphere of a late period. Compare these two items: The

Eastern and Palestinian Jews pray that they should enjoy the privilege of sitting in the sukkah that God will fashion from the skin of the Leviathan when the Messiah comes.[27] Leviathan is, of course, the sea monster of the abyss whom the Lord will kill. It is probable that the Leviathan is originally identical with the Babylonian Timat (compare Job 38, where it appears as a mythical dragon capable of darkening the day).

In this prayer the Jews express the hope that they will once sit in a booth made from the skins of that slain monster. Frazer gives a vivid description of the initiation rites of the Jabim tribe of New Guinea, now Papua. The principal rite is one of circumcision: "The place where the operation is performed on the lads is a long hut, about a hundred feet in length, which diminishes in height towards the rear. This represents the belly of the monster who is to swallow up the candidates. To keep up the delusion, a pair of great eyes are painted over the entrance and above them the projecting roofs of a palm represent the monster's hair, while the trunk of the tree passes for his backbone." [28]

Here is the primitive set for the scene, the hut in the forest, the trees and the palm branches. The impression the setting evokes is the inside of the monster which will devour the boys. We learn that they must remain in strict seclusion for three or four months, avoiding all contact with women.

The frightening idea of sitting in the belly of the monster is converted in the Jewish prayer to the hopeful one of sitting inside the skins of the conquered Leviathan forming a sukkah. But is the difference really so great? Is it not as though time has been suspended and we still live in the world of primitive men? In reality we have only returned on a spiral course to the point of departure in human evolution.

VI | The background

The preceding sections were mostly concerned with the original type of the booth, the primal type of hut whose late successor we recognize in the sukkah. We dealt with this prototype dating back to the time when Israel was, so to speak, still an embryo in the womb of the Semitic tribal mother in North Africa. We heard the modern explanation that the booths should remind the Hebrews of the tents in which they dwelt during their wandering in the wilderness. This was, of course, much later. Israel was then just born, was a baby, to continue the comparison also used by Hosea (11.1): "When Israel was a child, then I loved him, and called my son out of Egypt."

We did not consider the succeeding childhood years, spent in Canaan, during which the nomadic tribes became settled in the new country.

Our self-imposed restraint on the subject of the tabernacle in the previous chapters can well be compared to the technique employed by Rembrandt. The Dutch master chose a moment of animation or of groups in a certain situation and centered light on the salient idea in a single face. In his portraits he used light and shade, and centered the light on a feature that revealed the whole character of a person. Figures and houses were suggested in the shaded background.

Similarly, the central theme of the booth received the light in our presentation while the whole Festival of the Tabernacles remained in the background. Only occasionally a touch of light fell on the object of the surroundings, the whole feast. Do we now dare to conjecture, inferring from the material provided by research, what had once been the character of that festival, once long before it had its present character? If our guess is correct, the central feature of dwelling in the booths must take on the whole character of an initiation period.

Gaster points out that the descriptions of the great autumnal festival ('Asif) of the Hebrews contained in the Old Testament are of relatively late date and represent a stage in development when it had already undergone considerable adaptations and interpretations. The long Festival of Ingathering was broken down into a series of separate and independent festivals. Gaster observes that "when due allowance is made for these developments, it is still possible to recover, at least in broad outline, the original form of the festival." It comprised three stages, later distinguished as New Year's Day, The Day of Atonement (in its original form probably the climax of a lenten and penitential period), and the Feast of the Booths (stage of jubilation).

The picture that unfolds is a festival of long duration, perhaps of months, beginning with hardships (fasting) and ordeals, ending in a phase of jubilation. What now appears as a sequence of separate and independent feasts (The Day of Atonement, New Year's, The Feast of Tabernacles) was once a single long festive season, later broken down into three stages. I suggest that the primal type of that festival must have been akin to the initiation of the Hebrew tribes or rather of the tribal conglomeration from which much later the Hebrews emerged.

It is very likely that the Hebrew tribes dwelling in Egypt tenaciously adhered to their old rites. The Exodus passages reporting that the Pharaoh refused to allow them to go "to hold a feast in the wilderness" is perhaps a new interpretation of a pagan initiation festival.

I am not satisfied with the picture presented here; I know that it is incomplete and in parts dim and obscure. It has not the right apportionment of light and shade. Yet I hope that it is somewhere Rembrandtesque in revealing certain central features.

סעד

"THIS IS MY KADDISH"

1 | A childhood memory

When one grows old, memories of early childhood emerge, memories that have apparently been submerged before. One of mine brings back an image of myself when I was not more than five years old, on a walk in Vienna with my grandfather. As we were walking we met another old man—at least he appeared old to me then—with a boy of my age. This man pointed to his son and said "This is my kaddish." When my grandfather and I walked on, I must have said something that showed I thought the word *kaddish* a name. I must have thought the man had said "This is my kaddish," as if he had said "This is my Robert," calling his son by name. My grandfather then enlightened me about the word and gave me a certainly superficial and insufficient explanation of what *kaddish* meant.

Perhaps ten years later—I had in the meantime acquired a better understanding—I had another personal experience with the kaddish prayer. A friend of my family had died and I was called on to complete the number of men who say (or pray) the kaddish for the deceased. According to the Jewish prayer book, the kaddish has to be repeated for eleven months after the death of a parent and also on the *Jahrzeit*, the anniversary of the death.

If my memory does not fail me, I went for not more than a week in the early morning to the home of the family where I said the kaddish with the other nine men. I was then just fourteen. After the prayer we had breakfast and I hurried to my school.

What is the kaddish? In the present Jewish tradition it is conceived as a prayer for the dead, but this is certainly only the latest form of the prayer. It is simply a praise of God. Here is the special form of the kaddish said by the son:

May His great Name be magnified and hallowed in the world which He created according to His will! May He establish His kingdom speedily and in the near future in your lifetime and in your days and in the lifetime of Israel. Say Amen. May His great Name be blessed for ever and ever! May the Name of the Holy One (Blessed be He) be blessed and praised and glorified and exalted and set on high and uplifted and sung above all blessing and hymns and praises and consolations that are repeated in the world! May the name of the Lord be blessed from now ever for ever more! May there be great peace from heaven and life upon us and upon Israel and say ye Amen. My help is from the Lord that made heaven and earth. May He that maketh peace in His high places make peace for us and for all Israel! And say ye Amen!

In this doxology there is certainly no reference to the dead. According to most authorities the kaddish is "in no sense in itself a prayer of the dead, but the public recitation of it in this fashion by a son is regarded as a proof of the piety of the dead, as presented by a pious survivor." [1]

Only an understanding of the history of the kaddish can promise to tell us how its most important function became that of a memorial for close relatives. Before we turn to this, let me explain how that father in my childhood memory could have called the little boy his kaddish. A Jewish expert states that this late use of the word to mean "son" represents "the substitution of the function for the person." [2] For comparison he refers to the use of the word *lamp (ner, nir)* in a few Biblical passages.[3] It was the duty of the son to light a candle at the tombs of the parents—which custom still survives in the *Jahrzeit* light, kindled by near relatives on the anniversary of his death.

11 | The transformation

The old prayer attained its present use as the result of a long development. If we can trust the authorities, it was originally a prayer for the speedy coming of the Messiah. There was no fixed text to this doxology at first. Its Aramaic text was, according to David de Sola Pool, first fixed before the destruction of the Second Temple.[4] It received additional paragraphs after it became part of the synagogal liturgy (about six hundred years after Christ in the Palestinian tractate Soferim). There are various forms of the doxology and it has various functions.

The best-known function of the kaddish is as a prayer of the survivor for the dead (Kaddish Salem). The origin of this use is unknown, and scholars do not agree about its beginnings. De Sola Pool assumes that two lines of thought met to produce this usage.[5] There was, he thinks, on the one hand the response to the kaddish prayer with which the service in the synagogue ended. A Talmudic tradition attributed a high significance to this response with which the congregation professes its participation in Israel's religious faith. There is, furthermore, the idea, already found in the Talmud, that children who are living according to the teachings of their parents keep their memory alive. Later this was especially used in praying by orphans and was supposed to have redeeming power. The meeting of those two streams of thought led, in de Sola Pool's view, to the custom that it was the duty of an orphan to say the kaddish daily for the first year after the death of his parent.

Of a similar opinion is Margoliouth, who points out that the prayer was recited primarily after completing study of the Torah.[6] Since the study of the Torah was considered "exceedingly potent," the idea must have arisen that the departed might also thereby be benefited and that the prayer was then assigned to mourners. This use was already firmly established in the sixth or seventh century. The kaddish gradually became "an indirect prayer for the dead." Its original connection with the study of the Torah was lost sight of.

The great question still remains as to how it came about that this doxology, originally used at the end of the study of the Torah, became a prayer for the dead. We have seen the views of two scholars, yet our curiosity is unsatisfied. Their explanations sounded forced and we do not understand how praise of God became a commemorative prayer for the departed. Not even the interpretation that the believer should praise the Lord for the good and evil that befalls him convinces us.

A new avenue is opened to us by Salomon Reinach, who traces the origin of the prayer for the dead back to the Jewish colony in Egypt, especially in Alexandria.[7] This French scholar points out that the Old Testament is silent about prayers for the dead and refers to a medieval legend told by Bossuet. In this legend Rabbi Akiba, while walking, once saw a man laden with wood, and the burden was so heavy that it exceeded the load of an ass or a horse. Rabbi Akiba asked the man if he were a man or a ghost and was answered that he was a man who had died some time ago. The dead man was obliged every day to carry a similar load in Purgatory where he was burning because of sins committed in this world. The Rabbi asked him whether he had not left any children and what were their names and where they lived. When the ghost had given this information Rabbi Akiba sought out the son of the dead man and taught him the prayer beginning with the word *kaddish* (holy). The son recited it every day. After a while the dead man appeared in a dream to Rabbi Akiba, thanked him and told him that he had been freed from Purgatory.

To support his thesis Reinach refers to the second book of Maccabees dating from 124 B.C. and composed in Egypt by a Jew belonging to the sect of the Pharisees who believed in saying prayers for the dead. Hellenized Egypt, which sheltered and influenced the Hebrew colony in Alexandria, is in Reinach's opinion the place where the prayer for the dead— unknown to the ancient Hebrews—originated. At the time when Christ taught in Palestine, there were in Philo's estimate a million Jews in Egypt; they occupied, for instance, at Alexandria, two out of the five quarters of the town. From this time we have a series of Greek epitaphs from Egypt bearing witness to the custom of praying for the dead. There are, for instance, prayers to the effect that seraphim should grant the deceased victory over his enemies.

III | The return of the repressed

We have seen that in the opinion of the scholars the old function of the kaddish was slowly transformed into a practice, connected with the new cult of the dead. In this new use the living engage in actions destined to improve the condition of the departed. Margoliouth, who follows this development, conceded that a justified objection might be raised: the kaddish was connected with old ideas (as they appear, for instance, in the law of levirate): "one would have expected to find it in use in much earlier time than can be attested by the existing literature. . . ." [8] This scholar justifiably points out that continuity is "one of the marks of gradual development."

That is a good question and it can be asked in the discussion of the theories here mentioned as well as of Reinach's thesis. Was the influence of hellenized Egypt really powerful enough to overthrow the old function of the kaddish and to attribute to it the new function of prayer for the dead? If, for the sake of argument, we accept the other theory that the new function of the prayer goes back to old customs and beliefs, we do not understand how the new practice emerged. Which psychological agent was operating here?

It does not help us much when Margoliouth explains that such a case is not without analogy. He assumes that the idea of ancestor worship "was never eradicated from the popular mind" and it would "under certain favorable influences have been later on, freely revived under the form of kaddish hathom [orphan's kaddish]." Such a use of a doxology would be merely one more instance of the embodiment of old forms of thought in fresh and later shapes. [9]

Let me freely confess that this added piece of explanation

seems insufficient. Assume with Margoliouth that there was once a Hebrew ancestor worship that was later revived. How then should we conceive of such a new emergence? Where had the old customs and rites remained in the interim of more than a thousand years? And which emotional powers brought them to surface again?

Again only the psychoanalytic method is able to help us in solving problems of this kind. If we want to recognize which forces kept such old ideas banned from the conscious surface and which opposite emotional powers brought them again to the mind, we turn to examples from clinical practice. We seek the remote area of clinical psychoanalysis only in the emergency we have to face. No other analogy is available to solve the problem, and especially to understand the nature and conflict of the emotional powers operating in processes such as those in the development of this prayer. The particular dynamic action to which I refer and which I shall use for comparison is the well-known phenomenon of the "return of the repressed."

All psychoanalysts have many occasions to observe this process in their clinical practice and even in everyday life. The essential feature of the process is that the original drives that had been repressed, but which still remain effective, after some time return out of the repression. There is a phase in which those forbidden drives—for example hostile impulses—seem to have vanished, but then what has been warded off returns surprisingly and in a new form and has thus broken through the wall of the protective forces.

Here are a few instances of such returns of repressed impulses. A daughter is overanxious about the health of her mother and is especially afraid that the old woman could catch a cold. She wraps the mother up in mufflers and envelops her in shawls. But once the daughter overdid her measures of protection to such a degree that the mother was in danger of suffocating. The repressed hostile impulses against

the old woman had in this way prevailed. . . . A woman patient of Waterman had an extreme phobia against dirt and
stayed in bed all day because she had the feeling that her
clothes and the room were dirty. One day when her fear of
dirt had prevented her from leaving the bed she finally did
soil the bed.[10] . . . A man I treated had the obsessional fear
that his little son could hurt himself by running into the corner of a piece of furniture. In his apprehension he searched
for measures of protection from that danger by comparing
the height of the child with that of various pieces of furniture. In such an experiment he once pushed the little boy
against the edge of a table and hurt him.

The defense against forbidden impulses has in all these
cases become weaker and the originally repressed impulses
reappear in eruptions of the kind described. It should be
added that the emergence of the repressed into consciousness
is often favored by new impressions or experiences that resemble the repressed material so much that they can, so to
speak, awaken them. To quote Freud, "thus the recent material is strengthened by the latent energy of the repressed
and the repressed material produces its effect behind the recent material and with its help." [11]

Is this a key that opens the closed door and helps us to
solve the problem of the transformation of the kaddish
prayer?

IV | The ancient and the recent

The way back to our subject will be found easily if we remember several unanswered questions. How is the transformation from a praise of God (the original form of the
kaddish prayer) into a prayer for the dead to be explained?
Such a shift to another function could only be understood

if it were a regression, a movement back to an old, discarded phase. But if we tentatively assume such a backward move, do we not then run into another argument, formulated by Margoliouth? The anticipated objection would, of course, be that there is not the slightest trace of such a function of the kaddish before that time, as one would expect in cases of such gradual developments. The new function of the prayer could not have emerged *ex nihilo*.

That objection cannot be easily brushed aside by the general explanation, attempted by Margoliouth, that it would have been possible that the old ideas had never been entirely eradicated from the mind of the people and had been revived later on "under certain favorable influences." The process is difficult to imagine without determining the character of those old ideas and the nature of those "favorable circumstances."

On the other hand, Reinach's attempt at explanation is almost equally unsatisfactory. It goes further than the theories mentioned, but it does not reach far enough. Should we readily accept with him that the influence of a hellenized Egypt at the time of Christ upon the large Jewish colony in Alexandria was powerful enough to bring about that change of function?

I shall cut short this discussion and present my own theory about the kaddish as commemorative prayer. It has to be presented in a dogmatic form to avoid diffuseness and tediousness. We know that there was a kind of ancestor worship among the ancient Hebrews, originating in the common stock of early Semitic beliefs and customs. We restrict ourselves to references to the anxiety to produce an offspring, to have "a name and a reminder on the face of the earth" (II. Sam. 14:7). The levirate duty is determined by a concern for "carrying on the name of the dead man in Israel" (Gen. 38:8; Deut. 25; 5-10; Ruth 4: 15,10). Absalom erected a monument to himself, "for he said I have no son to keep my name in remembrance" (II Sam. 18:8). As Yeheskel Kaufman pointed out, the *name* was for ancient man "a substantial matter. . . ." [12] The deceased is buried among his people, his name is kept alive among them and still shares their vicissitudes.

As we know from Babylonian and Egyptian inscriptions and excavations, the dead were honored and were prayed to or, later on, prayed for—to make their voyage into the other realm safe. The Egyptian Book of the Dead, whose early texts belong to the Middle Kingdom under the XIth and XIIth dynasties, is perhaps the most significant proof of the intense concern of the old Semitic people for their dead.

Traces of the worship of the dead remained in the Old Testament, along with telling records of its vehement forbidding and condemnation.[13]

The final victory of monotheism and of the reform of the popular religion through Moses put an end to all those pagan rites and beliefs. The new religious regime repressed old pagan customs with terrible and passionate vehemence. The effect was, of course, that the forbidden ideas and rites were pushed into the nether world of emotions and thoughts.

Here I should refer to the comparison with repression in the symptomatology of the neuroses. Just as decisive repressions all occur in the early childhood of the individual, most attempts at flight from forbidden thoughts (this is the real character of repression) take place in early stages of the development of a people.

Repression rejects and keeps socially undesirable impulses and ideas out of consciousness. The repressed has a strong upward driving force and retains its tendency to get through to consciousness. It accomplishes this finally in the return of the repression under the influence of and with the help of recent material.

The repressed belief that originated in the ancient Semitic

ancestor worship achieves such a decisive breakthrough in its return. The old prayer for the dead, the emergence of their name, is revivified in the new function of the kaddish of the surviving son whose special concern it is to "carry on the name of the dead man in Israel."

We unhesitatingly credit Reinach's theory: the ancient repressed belief and rite concerning the dead was perhaps really revived under the influence of hellenized Egypt in which so many Jews lived in the first centuries.

Do not forget that this was not the first time Jews had lived in the country of the Nile. More than a thousand years before, Hebrew tribes had dwelt in Egypt and shared with the Egyptians the Semitic heritage. They felt an emotional and mental affinity with the Egyptians that ended only with the reform of Moses. The Jewish colony at Alexandria was, so to speak, a second visit in Egypt.

The essential process is therefore the following: There was originally among the Hebrew tribes a strong ancestor worship and devotion to the dead, later for the dead, as in ancient Egypt. Those acts and rites were energetically repressed by Moses and the prophets. The old beliefs and their underlying drives did not vanish, but continued to live subterraneously and developed some activity in the darkness. Strengthened and helped by the new sojourn in Egypt, these consciously forgotten and forbidden rites returned from the repressed.

As an effect of this breakthrough the new—or, rather, old —function of a prayer for the dead appeared in the transformation of the kaddish into a mourner's prayer.

I hope that this tentative theory tallies better with the facts of development than other explanations, since it also makes the psychological process understandable, especially through the comparison with the "return of the repressed from the unconscious." It explains, for instance, why there was no literary mention of that prayer and its function in the

Old Testament—the repression operated with full power. This theory also shows the nature of those "favorable influences" that were discussed before—the new *séjour* of the Jews in Egypt, which is certainly the country whose citizens had the greatest concern for the future life of the dead.

If asked to present other examples of that "return of the repressed" in the area of religious beliefs, I would certainly not be embarrassed. To mention only one case of the same process and its effect, in my Biblical tetralogy[14] I tried to prove that the prehistoric Hebrew tribes—or their predecessors—once had puberty and initiation rites that must have been similar to those of preliteral Australian and African tribes. I detected marked surviving traces of those later repressed initiation rituals in the myths of the Old Testament. Those vanished rites are not mentioned in the Scripture except in a distorted form which I could unearth and interpret. They remained banned and returned only a few thousand years later in the drastically modified form of the Bar-Mitzwah celebration in Judaism.

The new (or rather a renewed) function of the prayer for the dead was by and by changed into the practice of a commemorative prayer. As such it is also kept alive by many Jews who are otherwise alienated from their religion.[15] It is not even forgotten by those Jews who have deserted the faith of their fathers. A poem called *"Gedächtnisfeier"* by Heinrich Heine begins with these lines:

> Keine Messe wird man singen,
> Keinen Kadosch wird man sagen,
> Nichts gesagt und nicht gesungen
> Wird an meinen Sterbetagen. . . .

> [No mass will be sung,
> No kaddish will be spoken
> On the anniversary of my death
> Nothing will be spoken, nothing sung.]

The fact that death and the dead are not mentioned in the kaddish does not invalidate my theory. The omission rather confirms it, since their memory was once in prehistoric times in the center of the prayer. Every trace of the old Egyptian ancestor worship was energetically effaced by Moses' reform. Yet the use and religious function of the prayer speaks most eloquently in favor of the interpretation here presented.

Modern men conquered the belief in the survival of the dead long ago, as we are irretrievably alienated from religion. The son need no longer pray for his father. The most essential part of him continues to live in us. There are no dead parents.

THREE

STONES ON THE GRAVES
OF JEWISH CEMETERIES

1 | The living and the dead

The train trip from Berlin to Paris takes a night, but the
German army needed months before they could reach the
city. The French army had to be defeated first. Not only ex-
ternal hindrances produce such extended delays; obstruc-
tions from within can also effect prolonged procrastination.

Here is an impressive example: almost twenty years ago I
planned a certain book, the outline and structure of which
stood clearly in my mind. I even wrote about the project in
my book *Listening with the Third Ear*[1] and sketched there

the planned work. I started from the strange impression the many little stones left on Jewish graves made on me and tried in a few sentences to conjecture what the origin and development of that puzzling custom could be. It was an insufficient attempt at interpretation, dashed off and left unfinished in the middle.

Why these remembrances of things past? It would seem as though the wish to complete that unsatisfactory sketch was a strong motive for writing the pages that follow. I do not deny this. It was, so to speak, a moral obligation not to leave that sketch unfinished, but other motives were predominant and even more urgent. Among them the wish to discover what unconscious reasons prevented me from going to the end with my research project was certainly a powerful incentive.

I had not reread my book since its publication—I had opened it, so far as I know, only twice to look up a quotation. I had now to search for the chapter in which I sketched out the plan of writing that book. The chapter is titled "The Call of Life" and starts from memories of a June evening three years before when I had thought again of the projected book. I reported there that I had brought my collected notes with me to the mountain hotel where my family and I spent the summer. There follows the outline of the book and the remark that I had felt unwilling to write. Then there is a description of a lonely walk after dinner, of my thoughts and emotions on those hills. Then my final decision not to write that book on the relationship between the living and the dead, but to write another one on the emotional differences of the sexes.

Rereading that chapter, I experienced quite a few strange surprises. It was sometimes as though I was reading phrases written by someone else, an unknown person. Yet the same sentences startled me as if they were conceived by a part of me, a part I did not know. Especially there were two of these sentences, the one at the beginning of the chapter and the one that ends it. (Their significance will become clearer later.) The first sentence is: "No author knows fully what his book means to himself, from what dark background it emerges, why he wrote it, or what place it has in his personal development." Was this an anticipated idea of the personal decision to dismiss my plan for that book and begin to write on another subject? I believe so, and the final sentence of that chapter seems to remove any doubts in this direction and to establish a kind of subjective confirmation. The last sentence says I have not forgotten that evening "because also the books we write and those which remain unwritten are parts of our destiny."

At this point I should discuss the train of thought on which I reached my decision, but before I do this, I must speak of the subject of that book, of the theme which, as I said, "had interested me for many years," the relationship between the dead and the living.

As a boy I had once read some lines by the Swiss poet Konrad Ferdinand Meyer (1825-98), verses spoken by the chorus of the dead:

Wir Toten, wir Toten
Sind grössere Heere
Als ihr auf der Erde
Als ihr auf dem Meere.

[We dead, we dead
Are more numerous—hear our plea—
Than you on the earth,
Than you on the sea.]

This was a new thought for a boy, that there were many more dead people than living. It was an idea to ponder over for hours. The same thought recurred again many years later when I visited the grave of my father in the Vienna

Jewish cemetery. How many more generations of men and women are resting in graves compared with the relatively small number of living people! This thought occurred to me somehow tied in with the phrase "gathered to his fathers." [2] Preoccupied by this idea, I walked slowly through the paths and became aware that there were small stones strewn around on the graves. It is possible that I had seen this before, but now I paid special attention to it. Many years later when I looked at Arabic graves in Palestine I saw the same thing. I asked several scholars about the meaning of those many small stones, but I did not get any satisfactory information.

The source material I found in the literature later on was not very illuminating either. The explanation given was, it seems to me, rather superficial and almost certainly presented a late and secondary interpretation. The practice of leaving pebbles there "just before departing from the burial ground" is explained, for instance, in connection with the visiting of graves. It is interpreted "as a token to show that the mourner has properly paid his respects to the departed." [3] This cannot be the original significance of the custom.

There was no other way to find out the hidden origins of the practice than to enter upon patient research into the ancient customs of the Hebrews, their cemeteries, and their prehistoric burial and mourning rituals. One has to return to the pertinent literature—there are plenty of books and articles on those subjects—but now with the purpose of reaching an original view on the pebbles on Jewish graves.

11 | The pebbles

So far as we can guess the Semitic tribes from which the Hebrews later emerged must have had burial customs similar to those of other people living in the Neolithic age. Those natives of Arabia among whom we must search for the ancestors of the Hebrews were certainly as convinced as most primitive tribes that the attitude of the deceased toward the survivors is hostile. To give a striking example from the Jaluo of East Africa: when a person dies, all the people of the village begin to wail and continue to do so sometimes for days.[4] The same happens when a woman who had no children dies, but there is a remarkable difference. The brothers and sisters of that woman run to the body and stick a sharp acacia-thorn in the corpse's foot and break it off. The wailing stops then and is not renewed. In the opinion of most experts that thorn should prevent the dead woman, who is conceived of as envious and malicious, from walking and troubling the survivors.[5]

The fear that the dead person will haunt the survivors and cause them misfortune or death is almost universal among primitive tribes and was certainly present and effective in the Neolithic age. Among the precautions against haunting, the practice of binding and mutilation of the body was prominent.

People in different parts of the world believed that the soul of the deceased haunts the grave for a long time. On account of that continued fear, prehistoric men rolled great rocks in front of graves, so that boulders should prevent the dead—or rather their souls—from escaping and plaguing the living relatives. That elementary fear of the dead did not exclude love and longing for them, a cult of the dead—an attitude we would call ambivalent to a high degree.

The primitive boulder rolled before the grave of the cave also became a memorial for the dead buried behind it. Those ancient sepulchral monuments are most impressively represented by some of the grand buildings in the history of the world. Think of the pyramids of Egypt, of the topes of

India, of the mounds of Silbury and New Grange, the mighty megalithic circles of Stonehenge and Avebury and of so many dolmens and memorials from Europe to Africa.

The more powerful the deceased had been, the more that dark fear of him accompanied admiration for him resulting in the wish to erect an enduring monument for many generations. The grandiose pyramids of the Pharaohs form an admirable example of this emotional development. This contradictory attitude toward the dead, fear and love, still continues to live in us.

I shall not follow here the line that leads from the primitive rock before the grave to the altars in temples and churches which were, so to speak, psychological continuations of those early blocks rolled before the abode of the dead, but I shall return instead to the research into prehistoric Israel.

We know that burial was the regular form of disposal of the dead. As excavations prove, rock-hewn tombs, mostly in groups, and closed with a stone slab, were common. In ancient times each family had its own burial place. The cave of Machbelah in which Sarah, Abraham, Isaac, Rebekah, Leah, and Jacob are said to have been buried is a representative example of this kind.[6] The wish to "sleep with their fathers," to be buried in the tomb of the family must have been intense in Biblical times—as it still is in many Jewish circles today.

A relatively recent form of the primitive block rolled before the entrance of the grave is the tombstone that marks the dwelling place of the dead. We read on tombstones expressions of admiration, mourning and praise for the deceased. The other part of our ambivalent attitude is nowhere mentioned, yet it is still present. The surviving fear of the dead is still experienced, as the saying *"De mortuis nihil nisi bene"* (about dead people nothing should be said but good) suggests.

:

I shall use this place to insert some remarks concerning the influence of ancient Egypt on Hebrew customs. That influence has been mentioned in this book. I am inclined to believe that the burial rites of the superior Egyptian civilization profoundly impressed the Hebrew tribes that dwelled in the country of the Nile for several hundred years. The tombstones themselves are perhaps substitutes for the Egyptian burial monuments. We read that Jacob and Joseph were embalmed.[7] As W. H. Benneth points out, embalming was not an Israelite practice; thus Jacob and Joseph were treated as Egyptians, who were embalmed after death.[8] On the other hand, the regulation that all Jewish tombstones must not exceed a certain size certainly presents a strong emotional reaction to the Egyptian practice, according to which important dead persons got higher burial monuments than less influential people. The overreaction to such an undemocratic way of thinking was, I suspect, already the result of the rejection of Egyptian customs after the Exodus or rather a manifestation of the Yahwistic reform which we connect with the powerful personality of Moses.

Returning to the discussion of ancient Semitic burial ceremonies, I refer to the *Lectures on the Religion of the Semites* by W. Robertson Smith[9]—a book whose essential findings are, after more than seventy years, still not outdated—especially his discussion of sacred stones. Smith produces circumstantial evidence of the view that the altar is a differentiated form of the primitive rude stone pillar, of the Arabic nosb or the Canaanite masseba. Yet the sacred stone is more than an altar, "for in Hebrew and Canaanite sanctuaries the altar . . . does not supersede the pillar; the two are found side by side at the same sanctuary, the altar as a piece of sacrificial apparatus and the pillar as a visible symbol of the deity. . . ."[10]

I refer for details which make this development very probable to Smith's lucid discussion and only wish to emphasize that he offers an excellent example of a dual development from a single primal form. We shall make only a note of it and again focus our attention on those pebbles seen on so many Jewish graves.

We have seen that only superficial or insufficient interpretations have been given by the scholars for the strange practice, but it seems we are unable to go beyond their explanations. Our way is blocked and we are stuck at this point.

III | The psychoanalytic interpretation

The question facing us is the origin and significance of the practice of putting a number of small stones on Jewish graves. To solve the problem, we must find the unconscious powers operating here, because no conscious and rational motive for the custom can be found.

A comparison I once heard made by Freud will illustrate the difference between the research method, dealing with conscious causes and motives, and the psychoanalytical approach. A man who enters a dark room in which a candle stands on a table need only strike a match to get light. Let us now assume that there is no candle, but that the room is electrically lighted. It would obviously not be the appropriate way to achieve the desired effect to put the match to the bulb; the man must find the switch to turn the electric current on.

We too must find the switch, so to speak. The bulb is not located near the entrance of the room (or the problem), but in a remote place. The area from which I am choosing an analogous phenomenon is the symptomatology of neurotic disturbances, especially of obsessional and compulsive patients. This seems really very far removed from the subject of religious customs and ceremonies, but Freud showed us that there is an intimate psychological connection between the compulsive actions of neurotic patients and religious rituals, with which there is a great similarity.[11] He even called a compulsion neurosis a private religion.

Among the peculiarities of obsessive thinking is a certain process of distortion in which thoughts that are very important to the patient are displaced onto little details concerning apparently insignificant things. Here is an instance of such a compulsive thought or doubt displaced to the minute. During a walk a patient of mine suddenly could not decide whether he should pass a lamppost by walking in front of it or behind it. Psychoanalysis enables us in most cases to discover the important questions whose substitutes such compulsive doubts are. In this case, before arriving at the lamppost, the patient had been preoccupied by thoughts about whether he could surpass a certain admired man or if he must lag behind him. In the displacement onto the insignificant detail the vital problem of his assumed the form: Should I walk before the lamppost or behind it?

The psychoanalytical insight into the process of such displacement onto a detail as a distorted derivative of the original paves the approach to the solution of the question of the pebbles on Jewish graves. I confidently claim that those small stones are the last derivatives of the big block once rolled before the entrance to the grave. In a displacement to the detail they become substitutes for that primitive custom once essential for the burial. The many small pebbles form a substitute for the one big boulder. It is as though the survivor who had visited the grave of a relative, and so exhibits his piety to the dead, protects himself from their envy or hostility by putting those stones in their abode, preventing the dead from escaping. Psychoanalysts call such rituals "two-sided actions" because first the positive and affectionate feelings find their expression and later the negative, fearful, and hostile trends of the ambivalent attitude manifest themselves.

An objection that could be put forward to this would hold that the tombstone presents such a late descendant of that original rock. This is certainly correct, but I refer to the remarks of W. R. Smith, quoted before, on the altar and the pillar that stand side by side in Canaanite and ancient Hebrew sanctuaries. (The tombstone is put on the grave only later in a special Jewish ceremony called "unveiling.")

From psychoanalytic practice we know that important emotional themes find duplicate expressions.[12] Such double versions are to be found in dreams, in neurotic symptoms and other productions in which the unconscious has a decisive part. We discover a similar twofold expression in the dramas of great writers.

I hope that the foregoing paragraphs are sufficient to complete the sketch dashed off in *Listening with the Third Ear* and to arrive at the conclusion of an idea that first emerged twenty-odd years ago. It is not up to me to decide if it is right or wrong. It gives me satisfaction that I could bring it to an end.

IV | Self-analysis

Returning now to the theme from which I departed, I remembered that during the summer when I had anticipated working on the problem of the pebbles, I felt unwilling to write. It was more than the well-known writer's block. I reported in the book that my thoughts circling around that subject were diverted by all kinds of worries about my two daughters, who were then not yet twelve and seven years old. On a walk after dinner it had occurred to me that I wanted to write a book about the emotional differences between men and women. The wish was determined by the fact that this important subject had been neglected in psychoanalytic literature, but as my thought-associations revealed, the wish was also motivated by the anticipation that my daughters would sometime be swept into the vortex of sexuality. They would be young women in a few years and perhaps I would not be around any longer to advise and help them.

The decision made on this lonely walk in the mountainous country interests me in two ways. It has a Janus face. It most energetically rejects the intention to write the book on funeral customs of ancient people and turns with abrupt determination to the plan to write a book on the emotional variations between men and women. Both decisions were accompanied by intense feelings expressed in *Listening with the Third Ear*. The brusque dismissal of the old project announced itself in the murmured words "To hell with it!" and "Let the dead bury their dead."

I carried my decision through. Quite a few of the books I wrote in the following years deal with the emotional differences between the sexes.[13] That other book, originally planned to treat only primitive burial rites, was extended to the discussion of various subjects of prehistory.

The new project of writing a book on the emotional variations of man and woman had its roots in my worries about the future of my daughters. Yet this simplifies the psychological facts of the emotional situation. I had to admit to myself that the thought that my two daughters would have sexual intercourse with young men produced discomfort in me. Plainly speaking, I must have been unconsciously jealous.

This far the self-analysis contained in the chapter of that book goes. I said in the beginning that rereading it startled me. It induced some surprises. It was as though you see the performance of a play you had once seen before, and now new, unexpected, characters appear on the stage. The amazement experienced in rereading was not followed by confusion, but by a quiet and increasing clarity.

The first detail that became conspicuous to me was that I

had connected the anticipated adolescence of my two daughters with fear of early death for myself in my thoughts. They were then seven and twelve years old. Why should I be dead in a few years?

The second and even more surprising detail was the idea that I should call the preface of the projected book "The Call of Life," and the memory of Schnitzler's play that is so titled (*Der Ruf des Lebens*). In that play an old, ill man is left alone by his daughter who wants to go dancing with a young officer. I was clearly identified in my thoughts with that old, selfish, possessive father and my daughters were presented as inconsiderate and ruthless as the girl in the play. Did I compare myself with Lear?

Behind that screen of worry about my daughters another egoistic anxiety becomes perceptible: I am afraid I shall be deserted by them and die alone.

The decision to drop the plan of writing a book about ancient funeral customs and to write another on the emotional differences between the sexes instead thus had deeper psychological significance than I thought. The twofold movement—the pull away from the old subject and the push to the new one—was unconsciously determined. It was as if I had decided that I would not die so soon and that I would turn my interest again to the problems of living.

But why had I unconsciously tied the growing up of my children with an anticipated early death? According to psychoanalytic principles the anxiety that emerged here must have its cause in aggressive and violent impulses. It now dawned upon me that my two little girls must have sometimes hurt my feelings and that I had reacted to that mortification with violent unconscious impulses against them. Thus the death-fear, now emerging, is fear of retaliation. It is as if I would be severely punished for those repressed impulses and die early and alone.

Now, almost twenty years later, being seventy-five years

old, I am not afraid of death any longer, only of the painful process of dying, as perhaps all old people are. I could now turn my attention again to that dismissed project of a book on primitive burial customs, also on those pebbles I had seen on many Jewish graves.

If it is permitted to return in the manner of a rondo to the beginning of this essay, I remind the reader of the last sentence of that chapter of *Listening with the Third Ear:* ". . . also the books we write and those which remain unwritten, are parts of our destiny."

Can I now see things comprehensively—as from a mountaintop?

It was part of my destiny to write that essay on ancient burial customs in spite of my unconscious resistances against it. All's well that ends well.

FOUR

A STRANGE CURSE

1 | Another memory

The little knowledge I acquired of Jewish mourning rituals
was almost entirely conveyed to me by my grandfather.
When he was widowed, he moved into our home. I was a
little boy then and must have liked him very much at first.
Later on, I hated him passionately because he was in permanent conflict with my father, his son-in-law. Grandfather
was a religious fanatic and my father, whose part I took, an
agnostic.

The following reminiscence about a mourning rite also belongs in this sense to my remembrances of things past. They are, nevertheless, not things passé, since all believing Jews— and still quite a few unbelieving ones—today observe the rite I shall refer to.

In general Grandfather was a quiet person, but on a few occasions I saw him exploding in an attack of furious rage. Once a man must have hurt him deeply, because he flew into a savage fury and shouted "He should cut a *krie* to himself on his most beautiful *jomteff* [holiday]," but I did not understand what to cut oneself a krie meant.

It was explained to me later on. To cut a krie (the Hebrew word *keria*) means to rend one's garment as manifestation of grief and mourning after the death of a close relative. As a mourning rite the old Hebrews rent their garments, tearing them off as far as the waist. A number of examples of that ritual are to be found in the Pentateuch.[1] The first tear was made with a knife, the rest with the hand.

At the death of the parents, the slit is made on the left side of all garments except the shirt and the cloak. In mourning for other relatives the keria is cut on the right side of outer garments. The rending of cloth was later much reduced and the Reform Jews dispense with it entirely. Jeremiah foretelling the doom of the people predicts that they will not be buried; "neither shall men lament for them, nor cut themselves . . ." (16:6). When King Nebuchadnezzar carried many Jews into captivity, others tore their garments in mourning.

Cutting their own flesh and slitting their garments seem, as Frazer reminds us, an expression of deep mourning common to the Hebrews and their neighbors, the Philistines and the Moabites.[2]

Although several scholars disagree with this view, it is now generally assumed that the rending of garments is the later substitute for the self-laceration that is a mourning rite through a considerable portion of mankind's history, and was known among the most highly civilized ancients as well as the most savage tribes. Since Frazer has given full details of that practice (and I have treated it and similar rites in another book) [3] the psychoanalytical contribution to the exploration of the ancient ritual will restrict itself to a few remarks on a single aspect of the practice.

11 | Body and garment

When Grandfather uttered that terrible curse that the hated man should cut a krie for himself, the old man of course meant that the other person should lose father or mother by death. It did not occur to Grandfather that the original form of that mourning practice was cutting one's flesh. Anthropological or genetic questions like that were out of his line.

The interest of his grandson is now turned to a special side of the practice, namely to the displacement from the body to the garment. Observations in clinical psychoanalysis convinced me that clothes belong to that concept of the self we call "body image." The intimate psychological connection between body and clothing facilitates the displacement from physical laceration to rending one's garments, but does not explain it.

Support for this theory of substitution comes from an unexpected direction—from the understanding and interpretation of dreams. Freud has shown us long ago that the dream frequently presents nakedness in the symbolic form of clothes and uniform. [4] This symbolic presentation is not only a manner of description by the opposite, a result of the distortion of the dream. It makes sense when uniforms substitute nakedness. Are we not all naked beneath our clothes; are we not all uniform when stripped of them? There are even traces of that symbolic manner of expression in our everyday language. Don't we speak of the "birthday suit" of a person?

The dream symbolism confirms thus in an indirect way the theory that the original cutting of one's own flesh was later replaced by the slitting of garments found among the Jewish mourning rites.

FIVE

ASHES

1 | Another mourning custom

Other Jewish mourning customs, including shiva-sitting and meals after the funeral, deserve a great deal of psychoanalytic investigation. If I restrict myself in the following to an exploration of the mourning practice of strewing ashes on one's head, I have a special reason for this concentration. In the preceding remarks on keria (rending of garments), psychoanalytic theory could offer only confirmation of an hypothesis formulated previously by various scholars. The contribution had thus the character of a new confirmation from the vantage of psychoanalytic dream interpretation.

In contrast to the nature of that contribution, this section presents a new psychoanalytic theory about the significance of the practice of putting ashes on one's head. This theory arrives at an unexpected interpretation of that mourning custom, and the result could only be obtained by the application of the psychoanalytic method. All previous attempts at interpretation of that practice had failed—none succeeded in presenting a satisfactory and convincing solution of the problem. The psychoanalytic explanation will, I hope, do just this.

To put ashes on oneself seems to have been a traditional practice on various occasions. As Herbert Spencer has shown, the act often signifies submission or humiliation.[1] Even among primitive people, ashes seem to have been a badge of mourning. Some tribes in the Pacific states observed this ceremony: They mixed the ashes of deceased people with grease and smeared their faces with the mixture. The dirt was allowed to remain until the weather wore it off.[2] Covering oneself with ashes as an expression of mourning is as much a part of primitive culture as a splinter is part of a block of wood. We should not be astonished to find the same custom among the ancient Hebrews. To quote only a few instances, II. Sam. 13:19 reports that Tamar, after having been outraged and then dismissed by Ammon, was pouring ashes on her head. Job (2:8), who has experienced many misfortunes, is portrayed sitting in the midst of ashes. Jeremiah (6:26) describes the approach of the terrible northern conqueror and calls upon his people: ". . . gird thee with sackcloth, and wallow thyself in ashes." The ancient Greeks had the same rites of interment. In the *Iliad* Achilles, who has heard of the death of Patroclus, pours hot ashes on his head.

11 | Attempts at explanation

What are the explanations of such rites as covering oneself with ashes, and so on? Here is a sketch of the views of some eminent experts. Frazer is generally inclined to assume that the fear of the deceased's ghost and the attempt to make oneself unrecognizable are the main motives of many mourning rites, yet he reports some instances in which those motives are not predominant.[3] Among the Unnatjera and Kentish tribes of Central Australia a widow covers herself with ashes and renews this token of grief during the whole long period of mourning. If she were not to do this, the spirit of the dead man—which constantly follows her about—would kill her and strip the flesh off her bones.

With the lucidity that distinguishes him, Frazer points out that in customs like these the fear of the ghost is manifest, but there is "apparently no intention of either deceiving or disgusting him by rendering the person of the mourner unrecognizable or repulsive." On the contrary, these Australian tribes in mourning "seem to aim at obtruding the mourners on the attention of the ghost, in order that he may be satisfied with their demonstrations of sorrow at the irreparable loss they have sustained through his death." It is in accordance with this concept that the Aruntas and other tribes of Central Australia fear that if they do not display a sufficient amount of grief the dead man will be offended and harm them.

It is obviously easier to define what these ashes-ceremonies are *not* than what they are. Of the attempts made to guess their significance and their origin, none, so far as I can see, has succeeded. Most either did not reach their goal or overshot their mark. Such an abortive attempt at explanation appears in *Religion of the Semites* by W. Robertson Smith, who suggests that the dust was taken from the grave and the ashes from the sacrifices performed at the grave of the deceased. Was Smith himself dissatisfied with this explanation? He omitted it from the second edition of his book.

Even if one tentatively accepted Smith's suggestion, how should we conjecture the development of the mourning rites of pouring ashes on one's head and of sitting in the midst of ashes? Morris Jastrow courageously picked up Smith's suggestion.[4] Supported by new Babylonian excavations, he led Smith's theory to conclusions that were as determined as they were misleading. Jastrow's theory departs from the question *Why should the dust or ashes taken from the grave be put on the head of the mourners?* He tries to answer it by referring to scenes from excavated Babylonian steles. The mourners brought baskets full of earth to the grave. This earth was shoveled into a mould.

Here is an outline of Jastrow's theory. Originally the earth destined to be thrown over the dead body was transported in baskets carried on the head, as pictured in the Babylonian Stele of Vultures. When sacrifices were no longer burned for the dead, the custom lost its practical purpose. Among the Hebrews the custom was qualified so that the earth was no longer taken directly from the grave. "As a trace of the ancient manner of performing," the ashes were placed on the head.

The logic of this process is clear in Jastrow's eyes. Instead of supposing that the earth carried on the head was taken *from* the grave as Smith suggested, "it is *for* the grave that the earth is intended" and with the change in the manner of burial, ashes would be retained as a symbol of mourning. Jastrow is of the opinion that the ritual of pouring ashes on one's head is the derivative of an older custom of transporting baskets of ashes to the grave for which it was originally intended. The deduction is pretentious and highly artificial. Besides other objections, the theory immediately poses the question: how is sitting in the midst of ashes to be explained?

It seems that the mourning ritual of the ashes has not been explained by the theories that have been advanced. Yet in the areas of archeology and religious history there is no such thing as an insoluble problem—there are only problems for which no solution has yet been found.

III | The key to the problem

There is an applicable principle in the investigation of neurotic and psychotic symptoms: to take the symptom seriously, to trust what it seems to convey. This principle must also be adhered to in the psychoanalytic interpretation of the strange and puzzling rituals of ancient and primitive peoples. We apparently remove from this battlefield the subject of ancient mourning rites, when we turn to the emotional process we observe in the average or neurotic person who has lost someone near and dear to him by death. Freud called this process "mourning-work" and found its essential psychological character in parting from the object because the object no longer exists.[5] The dissolving of the ties with the object almost always takes the form that the relationship to the missed, the object-relationship, is replaced at least for a certain time by identification with the object. There are cases in which the mourners begin to resemble the lost person in one respect or another. I have observed some cases in which a woman deserted by a beloved man develops some character-traits she did not evidence before and which belonged to the lover. Thus it seems that this variety of identification is often an unconscious incorporation.

What can we learn from these clinical observations and experiences? We assume that the mourning-rites of ancient and primitive people must have had a similar character. They too show the psychological introjection of another person as a reaction to the loss of an object. Some psychoanalysts studying the mourning and burial rites of primitive people attest the universality of the process described.[6]

In the genesis of this process the ambivalence of the mourners toward the dead naturally plays an important role. The identification with him demonstrates not only love for him and grief at his loss, but also self-punishing tendencies originating in the unconscious death wishes against the deceased. It is as though the mourner confessed his previous death wishes and punished himself for them by, in a sense, dying himself. In this form unconscious guilt feelings toward the deceased participate in the mourning process.

Applying these insights to the particular instance of covering oneself with ashes or sitting in them, we arrive at the irresistible conclusion that the rites seem to convey the meaning that the mourner himself is dead, is covered with ashes which are synonymous with earth or dust.

Some unanswered questions certainly remain. Why ashes and not earth? We have no answer. Our conjecture is that ashes perhaps represent traces of an original form of burial by burning the corpse. There is, however, no doubt that the key to the problem lies in the mourner's symbolic identification with the dead person.

Nor must we forget to mention in this context Ash Wednesday, the first day of Lent, so named for an old Roman Catholic custom of sprinkling the heads of penitents with ashes on that day. What significance could this custom have other than the assertion that we are so sinful we deserve to be dead?

This, like so many other mourning customs, reminds one of the Biblical warning: "For dust thou art and unto dust shalt thou return." [7]

A FOOTNOTE ON MIRROR MAGIC

These essays on Hebrew mourning rites would be unsatis-
factorily incomplete without a few remarks about my last
memory of the grandfather about whom I have already written so much here. I remember well the scene as my father lay
dead on a couch. Grandfather came into the room murmur-
ing prayers. He went over to the big mirror hanging on the
right-hand wall and covered it with a blanket, but before he
did this, he had opened the windows. Emotionally paralyzed
by the death of my father, I only became aware of my grand-

father's actions later. I was in such a dazed condition that I did not pay much attention to what went on around me. It was only some weeks later that I heard what Grandfather's strange actions meant during that most tragic scene in my life.

In covering the mirror after a death one prevents the soul of the departed from being caught in it. This practice is widespread in Europe. Frazer explains that the soul "projected out of the person in the shape of his reflection in the mirror, may be carried off by the ghost of the departed which is commonly supposed to linger about the house till the burial." [1]

The common denominator of many such superstitions concerning mirrors is the idea that a person's reflection is his soul. This thought—common among uncultured people—lends strength to the idea that the mirror can abstract and retain the soul.[2] Whoever looks into a certain pool in the Saddle Island River in Melanesia is supposed to die because the malignant spirit takes hold of his life by the reflection in the water. The Galelarese forbid their children to look into mirrors, which will take away their beauty. The ancient Greeks thought that a dream of seeing oneself reflected forboded death. Frazer tries to explain the Narcissus myth through this superstitious belief. Even in modern Greece, sick persons are advised to avoid looking into a mirror.[3]

As Geza Roheim showed by numerous examples, the covering of mirrors with a cloth after a death in the house is a general practice of most superstitious people. The East Galician Jews turn the mirror to the wall, while the Jews in South Russia cover all mirrors in the house after they have closed the eyes of the dead person and lighted candles.

What are the motives for that strange practice? The explanation given by the mourners themselves is, of course, secondary and does not satisfy our desire for knowledge. The mourners declare the soul of the dead should not be caught in the mirror, but should be free to leave the house. In Baden, Germany, it was supposed to be a great mistake to lay the body out before a mirror. One must at least cover the mirror, otherwise very soon there will be two corpses in the house.

The many examples quoted by Roheim from many parts of the world seem to prove that the superstitious belief assumes that the dead person is full of envy and vindictiveness and wishes to take some survivors with him into the realm of death. These examples speak an eloquent language. Covering the mirror after death amounts to an unconscious attempt to get rid of the dead person. The glance of the malicious deceased should not look down from the mirror on the survivors. Hence the fundamental motive for covering the mirror is the fear of the all-seeing eyes of the dead who are still endowed with some terrible power as long as they are not yet buried. The foundation of that belief is, of course, the fear of being dead oneself—because of identification with the deceased and the fear of retaliation for our unconscious death wishes against him.

The power of the mirror is still felt in Hamlet's "to hold as 'twere the mirror up to nature." A survival of that magic power, once attributed to mirrors, still continues to exist in the superstitious belief that to break a looking glass means bad luck.

SEVEN

THE RE-EMERGING
MOTHER-GODDESS

1 | In a synagogue for the first time

If Hamlet had known the insight psychoanalysis has given us
into the laws of mental processes, he would certainly have
added that strange phenomenon to his praise of man ("What
a piece of work is a man!"—II, ii). The wonders of unconscious thoughts would have surprised him as they still amaze
us every day even though we have been familiar with that
particular "piece of work" for a long time now.

Why did an early childhood memory suddenly pop up in
my thoughts, which had been focused on a research project?

It dealt with the problem of what happened to the great mother-goddesses, common to all the peoples of the ancient Middle East, in the religion of the prehistoric Hebrews. There was no discernible connection between that research project and a reminiscence from the past of perhaps seventy years ago. Only much later, when my exploration had progressed to a certain point, did I become aware of a latent thought-connection that had remained concealed for weeks.

It was a memory: I must have been four or four and a half years old when my grandfather took me to a synagogue for the first time. I was not astonished by the sight of men in prayer shawls because I had earlier seen my grandfather covered with such a mantle.

What amazed me was the scene that took place shortly after our entrance. Two or three men went up to a platform and to a kind of recess or closet, the curtain of which they pulled away. After they opened that recess they took out a strange object. Or was it a person? Was it a prisoner who had been locked up there?

I am sure that my first impression must have been that it was a woman the men lifted from the closet. What I saw must have confirmed that impression: there was a wonderful long dress with many adornments and decorations and a beautiful crown on the head of the figure. Was she a queen? Everyone had jumped to his feet when she appeared.

There were, it was true, no feet visible, but the figure had a long dress as was the fashion in those days. Later on I saw something like a hand—a real hand—that seemed to come out from the dress, following the lines the men read from the parchment.

Only much later I understood my mistake. The closet was of course the recess, the ark, in which the scrolls of the law are kept, and that mysterious, richly dressed figure was the Torah. Naturally the boy was then too scared to ask.

The belief of the little boy who was fascinated and looked

at the scene was strengthened when he saw that the men were "undressing" the figure. They took her precious clothes off and removed the crown, while they prayed or, actually, sang. But even before that, they had done something which must have confirmed my impression that the figure was a woman, and a highly respected or loved one at that. She was carried around in a brief procession to the lectern. The men of the congregation near her touched her mantle with their prayer shawls (*talith*) and kissed them on this spot.

I still remember that when the men had removed the wrappings and adornments of the figure, they lifted the white scrolls high, showing them to the congregation. I vividly remember the feeling of sudden shame I experienced then. The corporal form of the Torah did not allow any doubt. The kissing had supported my belief: I had been a witness to the process of undressing a woman so that the figure appeared naked now. I had been present at a kind of peep-show, an exhibition shared by all the men present.

It cannot be denied that this impression renewed earlier attempts of the little boy to peep, but the scene in the synagogue was itself enough to convey that distinct impression. The physicality or corporeality of the Torah in its center was of great weight.

This childhood memory, whose significance became recognizable only much later, should merely form an introduction to the treatment of the subject of the mysterious disappearance of a mother-goddess in the religion of prehistoric Israel.

11 | The vanished mother-goddess

It is likely that for all the Semitic migrants who wandered from Arabia into the fertile lands of Mesopotamia and Syria "the moon was originally the supreme deity." [1] Even Moses Maimonides states that moon worship was the religion of Adam. The name of the moon goddess in ancient Babylonia was Sinne; she corresponds to the great goddess Manat in Arabia and to Venus, and Aphrodite in other countries. The moon was the emblem of Israel in Talmudic literature and in Hebrew tradition. The mythical ancestors of the Hebrews lived in Ur and Harran, the centers of the Semitic moon-cult.[2]

The moon did not long remain the ancient Hebrews' only goddess. As did all people of the ancient Middle East, they imagined that man had been produced by a divine couple as the product of their sexual intercourse. The Egyptians and Babylonians believed that man was conceived in the embrace of Heaven and Earth. In the psychoanalytic interpretation of the Genesis saga, Otto Rank arrived at the reconstruction that Adam was born as the product of sexual intercourse between a father-god and the mother-goddess Eve or Adamah (the earth). The myth-formation we know, the tradition that Adam gives birth to Eve, is a reversal of the original version that Adam was born from Adamah, the great earth-goddess.[3]

Adamah or Eve would correspond to the great mother-goddess of the ancient Orient, to the divine mother the Babylonians called Ishtar, the Egyptians Isis, the Phrygians Cybele, the Greeks Aphrodite, and the Romans Venus. All these goddesses were consorts of their divine sons, called Osiris, Tamus, and so on. After the liquidation of the kingdom of Judah by Nebuchadnezzar, the Jewish refugees in Egypt associated Yahweh with two goddesses. The name of the Lord was blended with that of the goddess as Anath Yahu.[4] When Jeremiah came to Egypt in 585, he gave the Jews there a severe lecture (44:2ff), but the men answered that they would continue "to burn incense unto the queen of heaven and to pour out drink offering unto her as we have done, and our fathers, our kings, and our princes, in the cities of Judah

and in the streets of Jerusalem for then we had plenty of vict-
uals, and were well, and saw no evil."

Only tangential notice can be given here to the idolatry of
that generation and of the preceding ones because our attention is given to the question *What happened to that great
mother-goddess of the ancient Hebrew tribes?* What, for instance, was the destiny of the female deity who produced
the first man according to the primal tradition? Did she dis-
appear? Do we here encounter a surprising reversal in the form
"La recherche de la maternité est interdite"? And what happened to other, later female deities?

Before we try to answer this question we hasten to add
that other goddess-figures of ancient West Asia were also subjected to changes of various kinds. The divine family (pref-
erably in triads of father, mother, and son) had various histories. There were in early Babylon, for instance, as many
goddesses as gods; each male deity had at least one female
companion. The city goddess Ninlil, the lady of the great
mountain; Nana, the patroness of Uruk; and others later
changed their functions. Some became "more shadowy reflec-
tions of the gods, but with little independent power, and in
some cases none at all." [5] There was, as Edwin D. Starbuck
once called it, a kind of "twilight extinction" of goddesses in
early Babylonia and Assyria and among other nations eager
to conquer the world.[6] There were various forms of the sub-
jection and transformation of the goddesses.

The strangest was defined by W. R. Smith: "In various
parts of the Semitic field we find deities originally changing
their sex and becoming gods." [7] It is questionable whether
such change of sex was really, as Robert Briffault and others
assume, the outcome of the struggle of patriarchal principles
against the survival of matriarchal society. In any event, such
change makes an odd impression, and it is difficult for us to
imagine its development.

But to return to our particular subject here, the vicissitudes of the ancient mother-goddess of the Hebrew tribes, we know (better: we assume that we know) what happened to her: She became a victim of the great religious and social reform we connect with the name of Moses. This tyrannical and intolerant leader of the Hebrew tribes and his followers banned the figure of the mother-goddess into the nether world. That removal was performed so radically that scarcely any trace of her previous existence remained in the official Hebrew religion. Occasionally Yahweh, the victor, took over her functions, saying "As one whom his mother comforteth, so will I comfort you: and ye shall be comforted in Jerusalem." Even the root of the goddess-idea was torn out: there is no feminine form of Adon, the name of the Lord.

III | A mysterious story and a mystery story

The idea that a goddess changed her sex and became a god is entirely alien to us, and we have no means to help us understand this transformation. There is a lack of communication between us and the mental world of the ancient Near East. To facilitate our understanding of the mentioned change and of others, I shall introduce here a comparison that will, in a lighter vein, prepare us for accepting some peculiar aspects of the problem. The question is not only how the figure of the mother-goddess disappeared, but also what happened to her afterward. We would like to investigate the circumstances of her disappearance, but we also want to find out if she turned up again in some disguise or other within the Hebrew religion. We know that she reappeared as the virginal Mary, the mother of Jesus, that this was in Christianity, a religion whose roots were in Judaism but which severed all ties with it. What happened to that originally female figure before that and what since?

The comparison I am introducing is with a mystery story. Here is the plot: The elderly wife of Lord A had disappeared. A sleuth, a figure similar to Agatha Christie's Monsieur Poirot or Inspector Maigret, whom George Simenon created, takes over the task of investigating the manner of her vanishing and, if possible, the task of finding her again.

No trace of the missing woman is discovered. Investigation brings to light the fact that there was a severe marital conflict between the Lord and his wife, who was unwilling to accept his autocratic rule. A young butler or major-domo called Moses, engaged only a short time before, plays a sinister role in that conflict. Lord A has made him the delegate in the household. Some rumors indicate that the Lady left after a furious argument with this major-domo—who ejected her and forbade her to enter the house again.

What happened to her and where did she go? There is a temporary suspicion that Lord A or this major-domo murdered her, but it cannot be confirmed. Could she still be hiding in some secret room of Lord A's palace? No one saw her leave the house. Since she left no belongings, it is as though she had never lived in the palace at all.

A long time after the disappearance of the mistress of the house, new persons appear on the scene: women who hold highly responsible positions. The detective who is still suspicious of the Lord considers it possible that one of those new women-figures is the Lady in disguise, but his suspicion seems unjustified. These women are not only much younger, but also very different in character and behavior. The unavoidable exploration of Lady A's life had revealed that she had had several lovers—there were even rumors that she had once been a prostitute. These new women seem extremely virtuous and have spotless reputations. Nothing indicates that there is any sexual relationship between them and Lord A, who is harshly puritanical.

The detective who quietly observed those women inside

and outside the house could find nothing that confirmed his suspicions. In vain the detective asked himself again and again: where is she now? There was not the slightest physical or psychological resemblance between the vanished Lady and any of the women-figures. Yet the detective could not rid himself of the thought that there existed a relationship between them.

So much for the plot of the fanciful mystery story introduced here for the sake of comparison. The reader will have guessed long ago what the points of comparison are. The Lord is, of course, Yahweh; the vanishing Lady the original goddess whom the Hebrews at first worshiped like other Semitic tribes—a mother-goddess, but also the goddess of love and sexual desire; the major-domo is Moses, the religious reformer of the Israelites, who banned the goddess as well as her divine son, ejecting both of them. But who are these women-figures who came to the house much later to hold mysterious and responsible positions?

IV | Personifications

After this intermezzo in a lighter vein let us return to the question of what happened to the missing goddess of the Hebrew tribes. For many centuries she remained lost and forgotten. As a matter of religious fact, she has never been heard of, only traces of her existence have been found in the early creation myth of Eve and a few distorted Biblical passages. There is no female deity in Judaism.

We expressed our astonishment at the fact that some goddesses of the ancient Semites changed their sex and became gods. Even more odd or freakish appears to us another peculiarity of ancient mythology: the personification of an abstract idea or of attributes of the gods. Yet those phenomena are universal in ancient and primitive religions and have their roots in the animistic beliefs attributing a soul to natural objects and later to the powers of nature. Such personifications are not, as one would assume, results of late developments. They are present among the aborigines of Australia and Africa and are found as well in early Babylonia and Egypt. And are they entirely alien to us? Do we not ourselves sometimes personify death and time? On the monuments of great men of the last century you often see symbolic or allegoric figures such as Courage, Virtue, or Victory, quite independent of the personality presented. Justitia, for instance, is still alive for us as a blindfolded figure holding a pair of scales in one hand and a sword in the other.

Scholars have described great numbers of such personifications in ancient Egypt, where some were worshiped as gods and goddesses while others had no cult. The same is true of Babylonia and Greece as well as of the ancient Roman civilization. The most frequently mentioned of all Egyptian personifications is Maet ("that which is straight or direct or what is the truth"). She is depicted as a goddess with a feather on her head and is thought of as the daughter of Re and closely connected with her spouse Thoth, the god of law and regularity. She had a cult of her own in an early period. We know that there were similar personifications in prehistoric Israel (for instance the Depth, corresponding to the Babylonian Tiamat), but they too fell into oblivion following the severe religious upheaval of Yahwism.

In the following paragraphs we shall be exploring the three most important personifications, all female, of a much later period, beginning perhaps after the close of the Biblical canon. All these figures present emanations or attributes of God, but increase in their importance as time passes. (They can be compared to the women with responsible functions at the house of Lord A in our interlude.)

The first of these figures is perhaps Wisdom (hebraic *Chochma*), known to everybody from the Wisdom literature of the Bible. It was always understood that Wisdom is of divine origin, but she developed by and by an individuality of her own. As Samuel J. B. Wolk points out, Wisdom made speeches, exhorted men to follow her if they would find God —"The adjective became a substantive." [8] A human quality became a distinct personality (Prov. 1:1-9; Sirach 24). On account of the rigid monotheism of Yahwistic religion Wisdom could never attain a thoroughly independent personality such as that of Ea, the Babylonian god of wisdom, or the Logos of Philo whom we later encounter as the second or third person of the Christian trinity. Wisdom developed an individuality but did not become a creator or competitor of God—"hypostatized, but never apotheosized." [9] Wisdom was identified with the Torah. In Ben Sirach Wisdom quotes (Deut. 33:4) and applies the verse to herself. (24,23)

The Babylonian god of Wisdom dwelt in the great Deep, in popular theology associated with the Tehom Rabbah (Babylonian Tiamat), but the author of Job energetically rejects the ancient myth and lets the depth say that wisdom "is not in me" (28:4). Yet *chochma* "was the first of the works of old" (Prov. 8:22) and "the Lord by wisdom founded the earth" (Prov 3:19).

A philosophical discussion erupted later concerning whether Wisdom was a being of herself or an attribute of God. She was certainly once conceived as something outside of God, Who consulted her in the process of creation. Is such "consultation" perhaps a later diluted form of a more vital participation of the wisdom-goddess in the process of creation?

The second personification to be discussed is the *Shekinah*, a female figure as is Chochma, but one who has quite a different function. *Shekinah* means the omnipresence of God. The word is derived from the Hebrew *shchan*—to dwell.

Philo assumes that *Shekinah* corresponds to *logos*. This is also the view of Maimonides.[10] The Cabbalists and the Mystics regarded Shekinah as the real entity. In the Talmud and Midrash the Shekinah descended into the Tabernacle in the wilderness in the form of a cloud. We find her again in Solomon's temple. In the Talmud, Shekinah appears as the omnipotence and is synonymous with the divine light.

The mystical philosophy of later Judaism assumed that there was first unity between Creator and Creature.[11] With the Fall of Adam there arose a barrier between them. God did not entirely withdraw from the world. When Adam was driven out of Eden, an aspect or emanation of the Divine followed him into his captivity. She went before Israel, going through the wilderness. In the same way the Shekinah follows everyone as long as he observes the precepts of the Torah.

The Shekinah also followed Israel into the Exile. It is said that she "always hovers over Israel like a mother over her children!" It is because of Israel that the Shekinah dwells on earth. The doctrine of the Shekinah has a central place in the doctrine of the Cabbala.

None of these female figures is comparable in impact to that of the Torah, the image of God, the creator of the world. The Cabbala explained that the stories we find in the Torah are subordinate to her essence.[12] Those stories are only her "garments"; without them the world could not endure her.

Together with God and Israel, the Torah forms the base upon which Judaism rests. She is considered older than the material world and was assigned a cosmic role as an instrument whereby God created the universe. Even in this thoroughly diluted form we recognize the primal female goddess who, with God, produced the world.

Shekinah, Chochma, Torah—these are the disguised, scarcely recognizable figures of the Hebrew primal mother-goddess. Driven out, they returned by a side door in order to

remain in the house—especially true of the personified Torah.

It is remarkable that the unadmitted cult of one of those
female figures is sometimes at the expense of Yahweh, whose
emanations they represent. I was once present at a heated discussion between one religious Jew and another. Impatiently
brushing aside an argument, one said: "Who speaks of God?
I am talking about the Holy Torah."

The ability to personify those remnants of the primal Hebrew mother-goddess did not perish even after the Talmudic
period. It continued to live in the artists who kept old traditions alive. E. M. Lilien presented Sabbath as a queen.[13] In
Heinrich Heine's *Hebrew Melodies,* Princess Sabbath is
praised and celebrated because she changes the doggish life
of the Jew into that of a prince every Friday evening. He
sings then the old hymn:

"Lecho Daudi Likras Kalle,"
Komm, Geliebter, deiner harret
Schon die Braut, die dir entschleiert
Ihr verschaemtes Angesicht. . . .

["Lecho Daudi Likras Kalle,"
Loved one, come. The bride already
Waiteth for thee, to uncover
To thy face her blushing features.
This most charming marriage ditty
Was composed by the illustrious Minnesinger
Don Jehudah ben Halevy.
In the song was celebrated
The espousal of Prince Israel
With the lovely Princess Sabbath
Whom they call the silent princess.]

This hymn, erroneously ascribed here to Judah Halevi,
was composed in 1540 by Salomon Halevi Alkabeth and re-

flects the old Cabbalistic tradition in which the disavowed mother-goddess reappears in another form.[14]

v | Return to the childhood memory

Even if the Hebrew names Shekinah, Chochma, and Torah were not feminine, one could easily guess that they are women from the descriptions we have of them. Their prototype, the mother-goddess, suffered a rude expulsion more than two thousand years ago and was never officially readmitted. In the best Old Testament fashion, even her name was expunged from the records.

Yet let us look at a few myths or tales connected with those substituting figures and let us consider the tales as definite evidence of their true identity. There is, for instance, a tale about the Shekinah. As mentioned before, the Shekinah followed Israel into Exile "always hovering over Israel like a mother over her children." In the Cabbala the Shekinah is called "the Matrona," which is itself revealing. The mystics predicted that in times to come, God would restore the Shekinah to her place. There would then be a complete reunion and the Lord would be one, and His name one. It may be said: "Is He not now one?" The answer is no, for the Matrona is removed from the king. The king without the Matrona is not invested with the crown as before. But when He joins the Matrona, who will crown Him with many resplendent crowns, then the supernatural mother will invest Him in a fitting manner.

The Cabbala does not consider that the Lord as long as He is without crowns has less responsibility ("Uneasy lies the head that wears the crown"). But now that the king is not with the Matrona, the supernatural mother withholds her crowns. Therefore, as it were, He is not one. When the Matrona shall return to the place of the temple, the king will be wedded to her. Then all will be joined together without separation.

It is easy to recognize that in this Cabbala prediction the primal mother is readmitted and the old Semitic myth of a sexual union of God with her has returned from the area of the repressed after many centuries of expulsion.

The other tale or simile will bring us closer to the quintessence of my childhood memory, especially to the boy's impression of the indecent "undressing" of the Torah in the synagogue. The Jewish scholars declared that the stories to be found in the Torah are to be compared to "outer garments," as Simeon said. Whoever looks at them otherwise, woe to that man! He will have no portion in the next world. We are told that one has to observe the things beneath the garments. The Torah has a body made up of the precepts called *gufe Torah* (bodies), and that body is enveloped in garments made up of worldly narratives. The senseless people see only the garment, the mere narratives. Those who are somewhat wise penetrate as far as "the body" while the really wise penetrate right to the soul.

This is the doctrine of the Cabbala and the comparison is, of course, meant only as a simile. Yet the word *Torah* has a double significance, a literal and a symbolic one. The little boy who saw several men take out the queenly dressed Torah from the ark and who looked, half-curious and half-ashamed, at her undressing was not entirely mistaken when he assumed that the mysterious object was a woman.[15]

EIGHT

REMARKS ON RITUAL UNCLEANLINESS

1 | What is clean?

One of the earliest memories associated with my grandfather dates from the time when my mother took me to the little town where her parents lived—Mattersdorf, on the borders of Austria and Hungary; it is now part of the Republic of Austria. Mattersdorf is near Eisenstadt, where Haydn was born, and could be reached from Vienna by rail in a few hours. I don't remember the journey, but I recall vividly the one day I spent with my grandparents, especially supper with them.

Mother had to return to Vienna the same day and was to

pick me up the next afternoon. Only my grandfather, my grandmother, and I were at the table. I remember that my grandfather said a few prayers before or during the supper. After we had finished eating, something happened that bewildered the boy who was then certainly no more than five years old. Grandfather turned to Grandmother and said casually: *"Mach den Tische rein!"*—Clean the table!

Without a word, Grandmother got up from her chair and left the room. I was astonished because I had expected she would brush away the bread crumbs as I had seen Mother do after a meal. But Grandmother did nothing of the kind. I did not receive the impression that she was offended or hurt by what Grandfather said; she simply left as if she had not heard his request to clean the table.

Not until many years later did I understand the significance of the supper scene, the meaning of my grandfather's words, and the behavior of Grandmother. *"Mach den Tische rein!"* meant simply "Leave us!" or "Go away now!" It had nothing to do with cleaning the table, but with the ancient taboo of menstruating women.

According to Jewish religious law, the menstruating woman is regarded as ritually unclean. According to the Talmud (Tractate Niddah) this uncleanliness lasts during the whole period and is ended after seven days with the ritual bath the woman takes following her period.

The menstruating woman was called *niddah,* a word derived from the verb *nadah,* to expel. *Niddah* thus signifies the state of expulsion. Under Talmudic law, a man should not pass anything to a menstruating woman nor she anything to him.[1] When women have their monthly period they should really eat separated from the man, if possible on two tablecloths; at least man and woman should be separated by a water bottle or a loaf of bread. It is recommended that they eat at different tables.

Women who know the date of their menstruation avoid

sexual intercourse the day before. When menstruation is finished (but not before the fifth day), they should convince
themselves by introducing a patch that they are again free
from bleeding. From this date seven more "clean" days are
counted—often tested by the patch to assure that all dis-
charge has really disappeared. Only then do the women take
the ritual bath (*Mikveh*).

The rabbis have elaborated a whole system from the Leviticus prescription (15:19): "And if a woman have an issue,
and her issue in her flesh be blood, she shall put apart seven
days: and whosoever toucheth her shall be unclean until the
even"—and so on.

A comparison between the older regulations in Leviticus
and the newer Talmudic rules, as well as the very expression
niddah, leads to the conclusion that the instructions concerning the taboo on menstruating women have been considerably moderated and diluted. At one time women must have
been separated from all men during that period, as they
still are among primitive tribes in Australia and Africa.
Compared with that "expulsion," still recognizable in *niddah,* the demand of my grandfather that his wife clean the
table was only a milder remnant of the old orders.

11 | Tabooed women

We should not be surprised to find the taboo on menstruating women strictest among savage and illiterate people.
Among the Déné and most other American tribes, "hardly
any other being was the object of so much dread as a menstruating woman." [2] When the signs of menstruation appeared in a young girl, she was segregated and had to live
in a small hut. During that time she had to abstain from
touching anything belonging to a man. She had to wear a

special bonnet with fringes falling over her head, as if the mere sight of her were dangerous to society.

The Bribri Indians of Costa Rica considered a menstruating woman unclean, allowing her only banana leaves as plates for her food and special vessels for her drink; things touched by a menstruating woman were to be destroyed. An Australian native who discovered that his menstruating wife had lain on his blanket killed her and died of terror himself shortly afterward.

The taboo on menstruation seems to be especially observed by girls at puberty. At puberty, the Negro girls of Loanga have to live in separate huts. When a girl of the Zulu and other South African tribes discovers the first signs of puberty she hides herself among the reeds for the day, so as not to be seen by men, and is secluded in a hut when she returns after dark. Among some tribes in the Lake Nyassa region, a girl at her first menstruation is kept apart in a darkened house. In a district of New Guinea, daughters of chiefs, when they become about twelve or thirteen years of age, are kept indoors for two or three years and never allowed—on any pretext— to descend from the house. In many parts of the world, girls are shut up by themselves in a dark room, often for months, on reaching their first menstruation. During this time no man, not even her own father may come into the house. If a father in the Island of Mabui were to enter the room in which his menstruating daughter was squatting, he would certainly have bad luck. Among the Kolosh Indians of Alaska a girl at the first signs of maturity was confined to a little hut in which she had to remain for a year. Only later in some places was the time of seclusion reduced to six months.

Father A. G. Morice wrote of the Canadian Déné tribes that in the eyes of these Indians a menstruating woman "is the very incarnation of evil, a plague to be avoided at all costs, a being with whom all contact, however innocent and indirect, entails exceedingly dreadful consequences." [3] The same priest asserts that the avoidance of menstruating Déné women is analogous to the Hebrew practice, so much so that were it not profane "the Déné ritual code might be termed a new edition, revised and considerably augmented, of the Mosaic ceremonial law."

What is the reason for this mysterious and overwhelming dread menstruating women awaken in most primitive people? Frazer made a courageous attempt at explanation in *The Golden Bough.* He sees the object of secluding women during menstruation as the neutralization of the dangerous influences supposed to emanate from them at such times. Unusual precautions are taken at the first menstruation, when the danger is believed especially great. These dangers concern those with whom the girls come in contact, but may also be destructive to themselves. "To repress this force within the limits necessary for the safety of all concerned is the object of the taboos in question." [4]

The mysterious energy emanating from menstruating women "is in itself neither good nor bad, but becomes beneficial or maleficent on its application." Comparing the taboos of menstruating women with those of divine kings or priests, Frazer states that "they are intended to preserve the life of the divine person and with it the life of his subjects and worshippers."

Frazer's explanation is clear and, as far as it goes, valid. It does not go far enough in the psychological direction. Only Freud's interpretation of the phenomenon of taboo reached its core. [5]

III | The curse of Eve's daughters

Among many peoples menstruation is ascribed to the bite of a snake. [6] There are images from New Guinea showing a crocodile or a snake entering or emerging from the female genitals. When a Chiriguanos girl first menstruates, women try to drive off "the snake which has wounded her" with sticks. Basuto girls, on the other hand, dance round the image of the snake at this period. In Portugal menstruation was traced to a serpent; a similar superstition must have existed in Germany in the eighteenth century because there was a belief that the hair of a menstruating woman, if buried, would become a snake. The Orinoco tribes assume that serpents try to have intercourse with women during menstruation. There is an ancient notion in India and in neighboring countries of the East that women at the time of menstruation are possessed by a malignant spirit in the form of a snake. Many similar beliefs were cited by Robert Briffault and I. I. MacCulloch.[7]

Rabbinical opinion tended to the belief that menstruation was punishment for Eve's transgression.[8] Salomon Reinach points to Genesis 3:15 (in which the Lord said to the Serpent "And I will put enmity between thee and the woman, and between thy seed and her seed; it shall bruise thy head, and thou shalt bruise his heel") and finds an allusion to an old myth of the origin of menstruation.[9]

It is remarkable that the legends contend that women were exempt from their customary ailments during the Hebrew stay in the desert, thought to be their reward because women were the first who declared themselves ready to accept the Torah.

Obviously the shape of the serpent was thought to be similar to that of the erected penis. Defloration led to bleeding, and menstrual blood was supposed to be produced by a similar wounding by a snake.

Reinach's suggestion with regard to the Genesis saga is perhaps correct. In any event, the belief to which he alludes was so tenacious that even now many American women still term it "the curse" when they speak of menstruation. The biblical tradition, and with it an ancient myth of the origin of menstruation, thus had an impact far beyond its influence upon Judaism. It also worked upon Christianity (and in this sense one can unhesitatingly assert that there are pagan remnants in Christianity as well as in Judaism).

From the vantage of psychoanalysis, that old superstition can easily be interpreted since we know that in dreams and fantasies snakes and lizards are symbolic representations of the penis. In this light, the myth of the origin of menstruation simply conveys the meaning that the girl reaching puberty is ready to receive a male and to conceive from him.

IV | Psychoanalytic interpretation

I chose Frazer's attempt to explain the taboo of menstruating women as representative because of his lucidity, although many other interpretations of that phenomenon have appeared since Frazer's outstanding work.[10]

I noted that only Freud's *Totem and Taboo* provides a satisfactory explanation. Although Freud only mentions the particular taboo of menstruation, his psychoanalytic discussion of the taboo customs paves the way to new insights into this special form of caution, avoidance, and regulation. Without applying the psychological results at which Freud arrived, the explanations of Frazer, Briffault, and the others remain, as it were, on the surface.

The decisive question from which one must depart is: What is the nature of that dangerous something that emanates from menstruating women, especially from girls having their first flow? This question can be answered in the light of Freudian investigation in a definite manner. The main character of the psychological situation which leads to the taboo is the ambivalent attitude toward the object—or rather toward the one action that one wants but does not want to initiate.

The character of this action of men toward the menstruating woman is clear: They desire to touch her or enter her, to use her sexually. The menstruating woman awakens urgent temptation and with it fear of that temptation and its consequences—punishment for having yielded to this desire. All this is unconscious, of course, and it would obviously be useless to ask the men why they are afraid. They would answer with explanations of a superstitious nature, the more so because they are entirely unaware of those desires directed toward the menstruating woman.

The nature of the avoidances and precautions taken against those mysterious dangers leaves no doubt about the character of the unconscious temptation. It is the sexual appetite that is aroused by the sight of her, and revived with every contact.

It is difficult to understand why menstruating women should stir sexual desires in men, because modern man would feel frustrated when he wanted to have sexual intercourse with a woman during her menstrual period. It would work rather as a deterrent than as a stimulus. In order to understand or at least acknowledge the possibility that a menstruating woman could be especially attractive to men, we have to return to earliest phases of human evolution, to an age when man's sexuality was nearer to the character of the heat of animals than it is now. Those subhuman beings who were the ancestors of Homo sapiens were especially attracted sexually to females when they were in heat. The smell, sight, and touch of blood, later on often experienced as frightening or disgusting, were very exciting for those primitives. I am referring to a valuable psychoanalytic contribution by C. D. Daly, who continued Freud's research in this direction and accumulated rich and interesting material concerning the origin of the menstruation taboo.[11]

The psychological quintessence at the root of the dread of menstruating women is thus the unconscious attraction they exert on men and the power of the opposite feeling restraining them. It is certainly revealing that girls who reach first puberty are considered particularly dangerous to men and are therefore carefully secluded and protected from every contact with them. The ambivalent attitude of primitive tribes to the sexual temptation provides the key to the understanding of the taboo regulations.

It is no surprise that in orthodox Judaism, which has unconsciously preserved so many pagan customs and superstitions, remnants of the ancient menstruation taboo also survive. Although no longer observed in its old, very strict form, but now mitigated, qualified, and diluted, the primitive fear of blood nevertheless remains.

ANCIENT LIVING RELIGION

1 | Unforgotten childhood memories

The scene is always remembered. Two things, that is, were
not forgotten: the image and a Hebrew expression. When I
call the scene to mind, I see my room in Vienna when I was
a little boy. It is night, or at least evening; I am in bed but
not yet asleep. My grandfather noiselessly opens the door
and enters the room. He holds a burning candle and goes
directly to the window. He pushes the curtains away and
leans far out the window, holding the light high as if search-

ing for something in the sky above—and I know (but how?) that it is the new moon rising behind the houses.

I pretended to be asleep, but I saw him leaning out the window praying. He stood there a long time.

I do not know how old I was when this took place, but I suppose I was at least four years old because I knew then that there was a man in the moon and I thought Grandfather was praying to him.

The second unforgotten element is the words: *Lewohnoh be kadesh sein,* the German-Jewish expression for the benediction of the moon in Jewish liturgy. (The correct Hebrew expression is *Birkat Lewana,* which means sanctification of the moon.) I must have heard these words much later, of course, because during the event I did not ask what they signified. Perhaps Grandfather or somebody else explained to me when I asked, later on, what that scene had meant.

In spite of the interpretation that it signified a benediction of the moon, I maintained the belief that Grandfather had performed an ardent act of worship to the planet. At the same time, I am sure, I wondered about it. If I had known the expression then or not too much later, recalling that scene I would have thought he was undoubtedly moon-struck.

The occasions when childhood memories emerge spontaneously later in life are psychologically almost as interesting as the emotional factors that cause their duration of maintenance within us. I vividly remember at least a few occasions in later years on which the memory of that night scene returned. The first must have been in my adolescence when I first heard the French expression *le moment de la lune,* which signifies women's periods. Another, later, occasion was during a performance of Richard Beer-Hofmann's play *Der Graf von Charolais* in Vienna. In one scene of this tragedy, the old President of the Court of Appeals speaks to his young secretary, complaining that young men are generally unmindful that women are more burdened than they. Woman is

> . . . not yet freed
> From those primal and mysterious contracts.
> Subject still to the same nocturnal planet
> Which commands the sea. She is with every full moon
> Reminded by blood and pain, like a tardy priestess,
> Of her task here below.

Again the allusion to the moon and its connection with menstruation. The old man reminded me perhaps somehow of my grandfather, although another figure in the same play—the Red Itzig—resembled Grandfather more.

Much later, in 1937, that childhood scene suddenly emerged in my memory on a night when I was looking out on the wonderful sky above the houses of Jerusalem. Was it that I remembered Grandfather, who had often spoken of *Jerushalaim*, or was it my position—leaning far out the window and looking at the sky—that brought the childhood memory back? Perhaps it was both.

The most recent occasion for this recollection was, of course, collecting the material for this book, especially for the sections on the taboo on menstruating, which the primitive people assert is caused by the moon, and for the essay on the vanishing mother-goddess of the Hebrew tribes. The earliest form of such a Semitic mother-goddess was perhaps the moon.

11 | The Benediction

What was Grandfather really doing there at the window? The child who thought that he was worshiping the Man in the Moon was, of course, mistaken—yet Grandfather did something similar, although not exactly connected with the Man in the Moon: he spoke a benediction for the new moon. He sanctified its appearance. He searched for the new moon first; that was why he had been observing the sky so systematically.

But what is the content of that benediction or salutation? In the Ahskenasi ritual, the benediction of the new moon starts with Psalm 150. Then follow the words "Blessed . . . who created the heavens by His word and the stars by His command. He implanted in them fixed laws and times. . . . He ordered the moon to renew itself as a crown of beauty for those He sustained from childhood [Israel] and as a symbol that they likewise will be regenerated in the future. . . . Blessed . . . Who renewest the month!"

Then follow several Scriptural verses, repeated three times. In these verses the hope for Israel's redemption is voiced.

This is, if one can trust the tradition, the content of the benediction my grandfather murmured that evening. The experts assert that the blessing of the new moon is an old custom.[1] Rabbinical explanation is that the new moon is considered the emblem of Israel on account of its monthly appearance. Like the moon, Israel has gone through several phases of persecution without being destroyed. The appearance of the new moon is therefore sanctified.[2] This allegorical explanation obviously represents a later concept.

It is furthermore said that "the periodical appearance of the moon, like the appearance of everything that is of benefit to mankind such as fruits in their respective seasons, should be recognized by praise and gratitude to the Creator." [3] The Talmud says "One who recites the benediction of the moon at the proper time is like one who is received in audience by the Shekinah." [4]

Such high appreciation of the benediction of the moon poses an interesting question when it is confronted with the fact that the whole older law, including Deuteronomium, ignores it. Some experts like Dillman declared the moon ceremony was so well known that the lawgivers did not consider it necessary to mention it.[5] William Nowack properly considered this explanation unsatisfactory.[6] He points rather to Julius Wellhausen, who assumes that on one hand the Sabbath had gained in importance and that on the other hand the Festival of the New Moon was purposely suppressed because it gave occasion for many superstitious beliefs and actions.[7]

Without being aware of it, we were gliding from the area of sanctifying the moon, which is a custom still observed by orthodox Jews upon the appearance of the new moon, to the observation of Rosh Chodesh, the beginning of the month, an official festival of the community. There is, of course, a considerable difference, especially important to the Hebrew scholar.

A few remarks on that festival are at this point certainly necessary. It is not the liturgical, but the psychological interest to which we are attached in this investigation. The problem we are confronted with is the attitude of the earliest Hebrews toward the moon and the later development of this attitude.

The experts[8] assure us that the observance of Rosh Chodesh, the first of the month, was once a major holiday, more important than the weekly Sabbath. They also say that this festival was a reminder of the cult of the moon god.

It is easy to understand why this festival of the first of the month or of the new moon was once especially important. The date of all Jewish festivals depended on the new moon. As long as the time of the New Moon was not yet astronomically fixed, the date was solemnly declared each month. The Sanhedrin, the great Jewish counsel, claimed upon the testimony of two reliable witnesses: "The New Moon is consecrated." Fire signals on the Mount of Olives conveyed to the whole country the appearance of the new moon. Since the Samaritans sent false fire signals, messengers were sent out later to make the date known. In the middle of the fourth century the technique of the astronomical calculation —until then secret—was made public. From then on the new moon was solemnly proclaimed in the synagogue on the preceding Sabbath. There are prayers for God's blessing in the coming month and for the restoration of Israel.

According to Schauss the benediction of the new moon which I saw my grandfather performing is a much older custom.[9] It seems that in the ancient days people gathered in the open when the new moon appeared, danced in its honor, and performed various ceremonies.

The moon knows its place and time. Men do not. Yet they project their doubts and uncertainties to the planet. Juliet asks Romeo:

> O, swear not by the moon, the inconstant moon,
> That monthly changes in her circled orb,
> Lest that thy love prove likewise variable. (II, II, 109-11)

The ancient Hebrews had no such concept of the phases of the moon. They thought her born anew every month and saw in that rebirth a good omen for their own restoration and salvation.

111 | The moon in Jewish legend

The postbiblical literature of Judaism, often called the rabbinical literature, is by no means restricted to commentaries and arguments on biblical narratives. Fancy did not die out with the stories of the Bible. Folklore, fairy tales, and legends of the Jews are to be found under the heading of the

Haggada. Louis Gizberg has collected those legends that survived the Diaspora from various sources.[10]

The following paragraphs are a medley of legends and stories concerning the moon. The purpose of this potpourri is not to illuminate but rather to illustrate the attitude of the ancient Hebrews toward the moon. Many revealing details from earliest times crept unsuspected into those late stories.[11]

There is, for instance, the legend that God spoke to the moon: "I know well, thou wouldst make thee greater than the sun. As a punishment I decree that thou mayest keep one sixteenth of thy light." The moon supplicated: "Shall I be punished so severely for having spoken a single word?" God relented: "In the future world I will restore thy light so that thy light may again be as the light of the sun." The moon was not yet satisfied, and said. "And the light of the sun, how great will it be on that day?" Then the wrath of God was once more enkindled. He said: "What, thou plottest against the sun? As thou livest, in the world to come his light shall be sevenfold the light he now sheds."

Robert Briffault concludes from this "strange dialogue" that in the Jewish tradition the religion of Yahweh displaced an older cult in which the moon occupied a position of greater importance.[12] Notice that in the story the moon is called *she* while the sun is spoken of as *he*. This is entirely in the sense of the symbolism as it appears in dreams and psychotic fantasies where the sun represents the father, the moon the mother.

Among the Jewish legends is an example in which this dream interpretation is directly indicated—a confirmation of Freud's theory of dream interpretation many hundred years before his birth. This legend reports that Joseph once dreamed that the sun, the moon, and eleven stars bowed down before him. Jacob understood the meaning of the dream because he, Jacob, had once been called the sun. The moon stood for Joseph's mother, the stars for his brothers.

Jacob was so convinced of the truth of the dream that he believed in the resurrection of the dead, since Rachel, his mother, was then dead. Jacob thought that she would return to earth. "He went astray there," says the legend, "for not Jacob's own mother was referred to, but his foster mother Bilrah, who had raised him." [13]

In other legends the moon appeared as the wife of the sun.[14] When God punished the envious moon by diminishing her light so that she ceased to be equal with the sun, as she had been originally, she fell and long threads were loosed. These are the stars.[15]

In the competition between sun and moon there sounds an echo of the conflict between matriarchy and the patriarchal order which became the foundation of Judaism.

In those legends we even encounter the prototype of such later institutions as the Sanhedrin, for instance in the story in which the determination of the new moon is taught. God appeared to Moses in a garment with fringes upon the corners and bade Moses to stand at His right hand and Aaron on His left. God then called the angels Michael and Gabriel as witnesses. He asked how the new moon seemed to them. Then He turned to Moses and Aaron, saying "Thus shall My children proclaim the new moon by the testimony of two witnesses and through the president of the Court."

Another legend relates that the Moon alone laughed when Adam transgressed. God grew wroth and obscured her light; instead of shining steadily like the sun the duration of the day, she grows old quickly and must be born and reborn again and again. And remember that the crescent was an emblem of the Israel that was again and again reborn.

The legends report also that the women refused to deliver their gold for making the monstrous Golden Calf, and God rewarded them by giving them the new moon as a holiday. In the future world women will be rewarded for their firm faith in God in that, like the new moon, they too may monthly be rejuvenated.

What is of most interest to us in those legends concerning the moon is, of course, whether there are traces of moon-worship. Not only did Terach, Abraham's father, worship the stars, Abraham himself called on the sun, the stars, and the moon god. A legend reports that he would as a young man pay divine homage to the moon. Then the moon was obscured and Abraham cried out: "This too, is no god. There is one power who sets them all in motion." In this way he found the real God and found himself.

We are at this point up against a question that is going to take some answering.

IV | The ancient Semitic moon-goddess

All Semites had once a cult of the moon as supreme power. When Mohammed overthrew the old religion of Arabia, he did not dare get rid of the moon cult in a radical manner. Only much later was he powerful enough to forbid prostration before the moon (Koran Sure 4:37). Before Islamic times the moon deity was the most prominent object of cults in ancient Arabia. Arab women still insist that the moon is the parent of mankind.[16]

Sir G. Rowlinson traces the name *Chaldeans* back to the designations of the ancient capital Ur (Chur) to be translated as moon-worshipers.[17] The Semitic moon-god was "the special deity and protector of women." The Babylonians worshiped the goddess Ishtar, who is identical with the great Arabian goddess and has the epithet *Our Lady*. (It would not even be too surprising to learn that the ancient Semites addressed the moon as "My Fair Lady.") She also has the title *Queen of*

Heaven, which really means Queen of the Stars. She was horned and was, as all lunar goddesses, represented as a heavenly cow.[18]

The Hebrew tribes, or rather their ancestors, were the latest wave of migrants from Arabia. The cult of their god was associated with Mount Sinai—the mountain of the moon. The experts assume that the name *Sinai* derived from Sin, the name of the Babylonian moon-god. In Exodus (3:1) Sinai is called the "mountain of Elohim. This suggests that it had long been sacred." [19]

In the Old Testament, which is a collection of much earlier, often edited writings, the moon appears as a power of good (Deut. 33:4) or of evil (Ps. 12:16). Traces of ancient moon-worship were energetically removed from the text by later editors. A few remained, however, and can be recognized in the prohibitions of Deuteronomy. In 4:19 the Israelites are warned: "And lest thou lift up thine eyes upon heaven, and when thou seest the sun, and the moon, and the stars, even all the host of heaven, and be led astray to worship them, and serve them," and in 17:3 the punishment of stoning is prescribed for the person who "hath gone and served other gods, and worshipped them, either the sun, or moon, or any of the host of heaven. . . ." The Lord predicts (Jer. 8:2) that the bones of the kings and princes of Judah will not be buried, but spread "before the sun, and the moon, and all the host of heaven, whom they have loved, and whom they served, and whom they have worshipped."

It must not be forgotten that Abraham came from Ur and Harran, the main centers of the moon cult. It is easily understood that it was difficult for the Yahwistic religion to cope with the still-popular moon cult of the early Hebrews, especially of the Hebrew women.

v | The removal of the moon-goddess

There were various possibilities of the removal of the moon cult for the officials of the new Yahwistic religion: full repression or denial of its existence; prohibitions and punishments; threats and warnings; and so on. These alternatives resemble the mechanism of defense psychiatrists so often observe in the symptom-formation of neurotic patients. There is, for instance, a procedure of absorbing the forbidden into the region of the allowed—or even of the commanded—by a process of displacement. To use a comparison, it would be as if members of a defeated dynasty are put into the service of the new dictator—as if they were willing or even eager to serve him.

The historical material of the development of religion is rich enough to afford us many instances of such procedure. There is the example of Mohammed, who wished to remove the power of ancient Arabian religious beliefs. He could not openly attack the old moon cult of the Arabian tribes and could not hope to defeat many superstitious beliefs by a frontal attack. The Islamic reform becomes, as it were, legitimized when it was spread abroad that the mission of the prophet received the sanction of the moon-deity. It was said that the moon had descended from heaven and had bowed down to the prophet. Another story, generally believed, was that Mohammed was transfigured in the rays of the moon, which penetrated his garments and filled his body with light.[20]

It is very interesting to see how the prophet coped with the great Goddess of Arabia whose chief shrine was the Kaaba at Mecca. The moon-goddess was worshiped in the Kaaba in the form of a black stone—which is still the most sacred object in Islam. Mohammed, who tried to unite all the Arabic tribes, could not or would not get rid of this symbol of the old religion. He kept this most sacrosanct object and to this day the pilgrims wander to Mecca and kiss the ancient image of the great Arabian goddess.

The Yahweh religion is at least a thousand years older than the Islamic, and we have only a few historic sources from which we could conclude how it got rid of so many superstitions and old religious beliefs. The procedure of liquidating them must have been similar to that of Mohammed, if less successful.

The old moon cult of the Hebrews did not invite, but rather demanded the intervention of the revolutionary leaders of the new Yahwistic religion. We know from the prohibitions set down in Deuteronomy and from the complaints of the prophets that the ancient worship of the sun, moon, and stars was well able to offer resistance and was more stubborn and refractory than the reformers had thought.

Proof is given by the fact that even today there remains a minor festival of the new moon. We know also that the original prayer to the moon was replaced by a benediction, a blessing of the planet. The crescent is saluted rather than idolized. The text of the benediction—as well as its rabbinical interpretation—speaks an eloquent language. Not the moon, but God is blessed because He created the heaven and the stars and ordered the moon to renew herself. The mechanism of displacement operates here in pushing the moon to the fringes of the cult of Yahweh, to Whose will it (or rather she) is subjected.

Did the rabbis not furthermore explain that the periodical reappearance of the moon, like that of fruits in their seasons, should be praised? It gave only an occasion to think of God full of gratefulness. The moon is not worshiped any longer, as she was in Abraham's youth, but her reappearance is only blessed *ad majorem Dei gloriam*. We follow the development from a cult of the moon to a salutation, which appears as a deluded and degraded form of her worship. In a similar manner, Christianity let the old gods pass by reducing them to saints when it proved impossible radically to remove them.

Yahwism kept the ancient Festival of the New Moon, but reduced it to a minor rank—pushed it, in a sense, to the fringes of service. In an inversion of Emerson's advice, the new leaders hitched the star to the wagon of God.

VI | Conclusion

Returning now to the childhood memory with which I began, I must correct a statement made there. I said that the little boy had the impression that his grandfather was praying to the Man in the Moon. This is an obvious case of projection of a much later concept into an earlier phase. I should have said that Grandfather talked to the Man in the Moon— which is much more appropriate to the imagination of the little boy.

By the way, we know that in later times the ancient moon-goddess was often changed into a male god or that the various phases of the moon had different deities.

If someone, after reading this essay, would ask me "What are you trying to prove?" I would have to answer truthfully "Nothing." It was stated and proved long ago by the historians that the Hebrew tribes, like their neighboring nations, worshiped a moon-goddess or a moon-god and that only the severe regime of Yahwism suppressed the ancient cult of which traces still survive in the Old Testament.

I did not want to prove anything, but I tried to make probable—and I hope I have succeeded, "with a little bit of luck" —that in Judaism today as it is practiced in the synagogue and in the home, a kind of diluted, diffused, and degraded moon cult is still perpetuated not only in the form of a minor moon-festival, but also in the benediction of the new moon. It is as if a kind of heresy or blasphemy had furtively sneaked into the service of the official religion. The ancient moon-worship is hidden under the cloak of an old ceremony. Here is a Jewish analogy to many cases of such disguised entrance of paganism into Christianity and Islam. Satan sometimes enters the church dressed up as a monk reciting the old prayers so well known to him. My grandfather, who made *"Lewahnah mekadish"* had certainly no idea that he committed an unspeakable blasphemy when he blessed the new moon. He was pathetically naïve, like most fanatics.

TEN

PRAYER SHAWLS AND PHYLACTERIES*

I | "They make broad their phylacteries and enlarge the borders of their garments"

In one of his sermons Jesus reproves the scribes and Pharisees for the hypocrisy and superficiality of their outward piety. "Whatsoever they bid you observe, that observe and do; but do not ye after their works; for they say, and do not"; for "all their works they do for to be seen of men: they make broad their phylacteries, and enlarge the borders of their garments." [1] There is no doubt as to the Saviour's meaning in uttering this reproach.

* First published in German in *Imago* [edited by Sigmund Freud], XVI (1930).

The exhibition of piety, the demonstrative character of religious exercises are indicated by a representative example. The Pharisees—so the Lord declares—make the bands or thongs of their prayer satchels, the *tephillin,* broad and conspicuous. They enlarge the borders or fringes the Jews wear upon their garments, in obedience to the commandment, to demonstrate their loyal observance of the Law. The wearing of these prayer satchels and fringes was a religious custom which in the Saviour's time was conscientiously observed by every Jew. The Saviour did not attack this ritual as such, only its exaggerations and aberrations.

He himself wore such hems or borders, in compliance with the Law, and the Gospel according to St. Matthew tells us that those who believed in him held that there was healing in the touch of these hems or fringes (Hebrew: *zizzith*). The people of Genesareth asked that the sick should be allowed to touch the zizzith of his garment. Those who touched it were made whole.[2] "A woman who was diseased with an issue of blood twelve years came behind him and touched the hem of his garment. . . . Jesus turned him about, and when he saw her, he said: Daughter, be of good comfort; thy faith hath made thee whole. And the woman was made whole. . . ."

The problem of such singular therapy naturally excites our curiosity. We should also like to know more of the peculiar objects which were of such great religious significance. It is not difficult to satisfy our curiosity. We have only to observe a pious Jew as he repeats his morning prayer. We shall then have an excellent opportunity of obtaining a clear notion of this religious practice. We see how the pious Jew throws a cloth like a shawl, called the *tallith,* over his head and shoulders. We note the four tassels at the corners of this article of clothing, and we see that thongs on which little satchels are fastened are wound in a special manner about the left arm and bound upon the forehead.

Although these ceremonial objects may have altered a bit in shape, they are essentially what they were in the days when the Lord was wandering in the hills of Galilee. They have the same function today they had twenty centuries ago, when Jesus brought mankind the joyful news of imminent salvation.

To us these objects appear no less peculiar than the praying gloves, prayer mills, and prayer pennants of the peoples of the Far East. Let us first of all consider the combination of the satchels and thongs. Actually, we have here two fairly similar objects, one of which is bound on the left arm, the other on the forehead. The head tephillah (Hebrew: *schel rosch*) consists of a leather box made from the hide of a ritually clean animal,[3] and fastened by means of leather thongs. This little black leather box has four compartments. In each is placed a copy of certain passages of the Bible, written on a specially prepared vellum. On one of the outer sides of this box one can see the letter *Schin,* with three teeth; on the opposite side is the same letter with four teeth. This four-cell box is sewn to his leather support with twelve stitches of the sinew of a ritually clean animal.[4]

These stitches, according to tradition, represent the twelve tribes of Israel. The thongs which fasten this head tephillah are bound round the head in such a manner that the box rests on the edge of the scalp, between the eyes. At the back of the neck the looped thongs form the Hebrew letter *Daleth.* This, with the letter *Schin* (on the outside of the box) and the letter *Jod,* which is formed by the thongs of the hand tephillah, spells the name of God—*Schaddai* (Almighty).

The sacred character of the tephillah boxes is apparent from the special prescriptions for their manufacture. The strips of parchment within them must be of a special kind; the Assyrian script on the strips must be written with extraordinary calligraphic and masoretic exactitude. Before the scribe begins his work he must solemnly proclaim: "I am writing this for the holiness of the Tephillin."

If he omits even one letter the whole inscription is worthless. The verse of Scripture which he has to write must not be written from memory, but must be copied from the roll of the Law. Every letter must be particularly clear; none can be out of line with the rest; none is to overlap or rise higher than another letter. A definite space must be left between the letters, and between the individual words, lines, and verses.[5]

The scribe must write the name of God—and only Jews may write these tephillah verses—with special reverence and a sense of its exalted significance. The injunction to the effect that the writer's attention must not be diverted during his labor is so imperative that even were he greeted by a king he would be forbidden to respond to the greeting.[6]

The text which is recorded with such special precautions on the parchment consists of four passages of the Bible:

1. (Exod. 13:1-10) "And the Lord spake unto Moses, saying: Sanctify unto me all the firstborn, whatsoever openeth the womb among the children of Israel, both of man and beast; it is mine. And Moses said unto the people: Remember this day, in which ye came out from Egypt, out of the house of bondage, for by the strength of hand the Lord brought you out from this place; there shall no leavened bread be eaten. This day came ye out, in the month Abib. And it shall be, when the Lord shall bring thee into the land of the Canaanites, and the Hittites, and the Amorites, and the Hivites, and the Jebusites, which he sware unto thy fathers to give thee, a land flowing with milk and honey, that thou shalt keep this service in their mouth. Seven days thou shalt eat unleavened bread, and in the seventh day shall be a feast to the Lord. Unleavened bread shall be eaten seven days; and there shall no leavened bread be seen with thee, neither shall there leaven be seen with thee in all thy quar-

ters. And thou shalt show thy son in that day, saying, This is done because of that which the Lord did unto me when I came forth out of Egypt. And it shall be for a sign onto thee upon thine hand, and for a memorial between thine eyes, that the Lord's law may be in thy mouth; for with a strong hand hath the Lord brought thee out of Egypt. Thou shalt therefore keep this ordinance in his season from year to year."

2. (Exod. 13:11-16) "And it shall be, when the Lord shall bring thee in into the land of the Canaanites, as he sware unto thee and thy fathers, and shall give it thee, that thou shalt set apart unto the Lord all that openeth the matrix, and every firstling that cometh of a beast which thou hast; the males shall be the Lord's. And every firstling of an ass thou shalt redeem with a lamb; and if thou will not redeem it, then thou shalt break his neck; and all the first-born of man among thy children shalt thou redeem. And it shall be when thy son asketh thee in time to come, saying: What is this? that thou shalt say unto him: By the strength of hand the Lord brought us out from Egypt, from the house of bondage. And it came to pass, when Pharaoh would hardly let us go, that the Lord slew all the firstborn in the land of Egypt, both the first-born of man and the first-born of beast; therefore I sacrifice to the Lord all that openeth the matrix, being males; but all the firstborn of my children I redeem. And it shall be for a token upon thine hand, and for frontlets between thine eyes; for by strength of hand the lord brought us out of Egypt."

3. (Deut. 6:4-9) "Hear, O Israel; The Lord our God is one Lord: And thou shalt love the Lord thy God with all thine heart and with all thy soul and with all thy might. And these words, which I command thee this day, shall be in thine heart: And thou shalt teach them diligently unto thy children, and shalt talk of them when thou sittest in thine house, and when thou walkest by the way, and when thou

liest down, and when thou risest up. And thou shalt bind them for a sign upon thy hand, and they shall be as frontlets between thine eyes. And thou shalt write them upon the posts of thy house, and on thy gates."

4. (Deut. 11:13-21) "And it shall come to pass, if ye shall hearken diligently unto my commandments which I command to you this day, to love the Lord your God, and to serve him with all your heart and all your soul, that I will give you the rain of your land in his due season, the first rain, and the latter rain, that thou mayest gather in thy corn and thy wine and thine oil. And I will send grass in thy fields for thy cattle, that thou mayest eat, and be full. Take heed to yourselves, that your heart be not deceived, and ye turn aside, and serve other gods, and worship them; and then the Lord's wrath be kindled against you, and he shut up the heaven, that there be no rain, and that the land yield not her fruit; and lest ye perish quickly from off the good land which the Lord giveth you. Therefore ye shall lay up these my words in your heart and in your soul, and bind them for a sign upon your hand, that they may be as frontlets between your eyes. And ye shall teach them your children, speaking of them when thou sittest in thine house, and when thou walkest by the way, and when thou liest down, and when thou risest up. And thou shalt write them upon the door posts of thine house, and upon thy gates. That your days may be multiplied, and the days of your children, in the land which the Lord sware unto your fathers to give them, as the days of heaven upon the earth."

It should be mentioned that there were prolonged discussions among the Talmudic commentators, going into all manner of detail, as to the arrangement of these four passages of the Bible; that is, their arrangement on the parchment strips of the tephillin. Thus the highly respected Rabbi Tam decided in favor of one arrangement, while the no less respected Rabbi Raschi recommended a different order.[7] This slight uncertainty, which is not without symptomatic significance although it refers only to the order of the last two passages of Scripture, finds expression in the fact that in many tephillin rolls the order prescribed by Tam is followed, and in others that favored by Raschi.

We note, moreover, that many pious Jews, unable to decide whether they should follow Rabbi Tam or Rabbi Raschi, have hit upon this method of ensuring that they have fulfilled their religious duty. They wear two head tephillin, one of which is arranged in accordance with Raschi's prescription, while the other observes the order favored by Tam.

These four passages of Scripture, which in the head tephillah are inscribed upon four rolls of parchment, are compressed into one roll in the hand tephillah, which is only about half the size of the head tephillah. The little box of the hand tephillah is fastened with a long leather thong, which is wound upon the left arm. The hand tephillah is adjusted first, in such a way that the box lies on the inner side of the left arm, under the joint.

This position, in which the tephillah is carried near the heart, is in fulfillment of the rabbinical interpretation of the admonition contained in Deut. 11:18, that "ye shall lay up these words in your heart . . . and bind them for a sign upon your hand." When the little box is fastened upon the bare arm the thong, which is passed through a loop, is first of all wound three times about the arm. At the same time this prayer is recited: "Praised be thou, Lord our God, king of the world, who hast hallowed us by thy commandments and hast bidden us to wear the tephillin." The thong is then wound three times about the arm in such a way that its convolutions form the four-branched Hebrew letter *Schin.*

The head tephillah is then placed in the middle of the forehead, and a blessing is invoked.[8] The thong of the hand tephillah is then wound three times about the middle finger, so that it once again forms a letter *Schin*, while a short length of the thong is left hanging down. While the thong is being wound around the hand, these words are recited: "And I will betroth thee unto me in righteousness, and in judgment, and in loving kindness and in mercies; I will even betroth thee unto me in faithfulness; and thou shalt know the Lord." [9] After divine service the thong is unwound from the middle finger. Then the head tephillah is removed, and finally the hand phylactery. The tephillin are then kissed and laid aside in a special bag or satchel.

Originally the tephillin were worn all day (but not during the night).[10] Now they are put on during the morning worship only, except on Sabbath and on holidays.[11] It is the religious obligation of every Jew to put on the tephillin daily after he has reached the age of thirteen years and a day.

We now have a fair notion of the objects for whose exaggerated dimensions the Saviour so sternly reproved the scribes and Pharisees. The other object mentioned by the Lord, and which He Himself wore, as the Gospel records, is still in daily ritual employment among Israelites. We see the fringes concerning whose dimensions the Saviour of the world was so indignant, on the prayer shawl which every male adult Jew has to wear during his prescribed devotions.

This prayer shawl is known as the *tallith*. It is a large, white, quadrangular cloth of sheep's or lamb's wool; it may be of silk. The silken shawls will be prized as more valuable, but pious worshipers will prefer the woolen shawl, especially if its wool is that of the lambs of the Holy Land. The tallith is drawn over the head so that it covers the forehead and the back of the head, while its four corners hang loosely upon the shoulders. The four tassels which we see on these corners, and to which Jesus referred in his sermon, are known as *zizzith*.[12]

These tassels—called *Laepplein* (lappets) in Luther's translation—consist of four white and four blue threads of the same material as the tallith. The rabbinical prescriptions relating to the zizzith are marked by a characteristic minuteness and precision which deal exhaustively with every detail; in fact, they fill many pages.

Of the eight threads which form each tassel, one is longer than the rest; it is known as the servant, *schammish*. After the zizzith are fastened to the shawl, this schammisch enters the action. It is bound first seven times and then eight times round the other threads, a double knot is tied. Finally it is wound thirteen times round the rest, and again a knot is tied.

This sequence of threads and knots has been compared with the knot-writing of ancient civilizations—for example, the *quipus* of the Peruvians. As a matter of fact, the medieval Jewish mystics attributed many secret meanings to the numbers of the windings and of the knots. One of these interpretations conceives the whole as a symbol of the Torah: the numerical value of the letters of the word *zizzith* is 600. If we add the eight threads and the five knots we get 613, which according to rabbinical calculations is the precise number of the positive (248) and negative (365) prescriptions of the Law. According to another version, the numerical value of the knots and windings gives us the words *jahwe echod*—Yahveh alone (is God). There are many other speculations of this kind. The one thing they have in common is the connection between the zizzith and belief in God and the Law. The wearing of the zizzith was often regarded as equal in importance to the observance of all the laws.

These zizzith, however, are found not only on the special prayer shawl, the tallith, but also on another ritual article of clothing, which may be described as a sort of miniature tallith. Actually this article is known as *tallith kothen,* "the little tallith," in opposition to the *tallith godel,* "the large tallith." Another and frequently used name for the prayer shawl is *arba kamphot*.

While the tallith is worn only during prayer, this particular article is worn all day by pious Jews. It is simply a square of cloth that covers the breast and back and is worn under the outer garments. This shawl is slightly different in shape from the longer tallith, but like the latter it has the zizzith affixed to its four corners.

This twofold use of tallith can hardly be explained by the historical development of Jewish dress. In ancient times the Hebrews wore a large piece of cloth not unlike the Arab burnoose;[13] it wrapped the whole body, and was probably used also as a nightdress. The usual tassels or "fringes" on the corners of the garment are prescribed by the Priestly Codex. These zizzith on the outer garment, which was so much larger than the later tallith, must have been (as we learn from Jesus' sermon) much larger and much more conspicuous than the tassels which we may see today on the ritual garment. The woman who was suffering from an issue of blood laid hold upon the Saviour's zizzith in the midst of the people.

As time elapsed the Jews wore clothing more like the garb of foreign peoples. The tassels on the outer garment were recognized as Jewish peculiarities. As the hatred for the Jewish people increased it became advisable to conceal them. This explains the use of the tasseled tallith which was worn only during the morning prayer, and the origin of the special article of clothing which was worn under the outer garments. Or so the scholars tell us. No doubt their explanation is correct, yet it surely does not reveal all the essential motives of the development.

As the tallith is put on, the prayer is spoken: "Praised be thou, Lord our God, king of the world, who has hallowed us by thy commandments and hast bidden us to wear garments with the zizzith thereon." As the tephillin are kissed, so the zizzith are kissed when the tallith is put on or removed. This the pious do to fulfill the commandment: "Ye shall look upon them."

There was an embittered discussion between the Tal-

mudic schools of the Rabbi Hillel and the Rabbi Schamnai
concerning whether the tallith had to be worn by night as well
as by day. It was decided that this was not necessary, since the
darkness made it impossible to obey the injunction to look
upon the zizzith and in so doing call to mind the commandments of God. The pious Jew is forbidden to sell such a garment provided with tassels to anyone who is not a Jew, un-
less the zizzith are first removed.

11 | The religious significance of the phylacteries

The natural method of learning anything as to the significance of these mysterious religious objects is to apply to the
Jewish authorities. One would expect that the Talmud, the
vast, comprehensive lawbook of the Jewish religion, would
give us exhaustive information. As a matter of fact, the religious literature of Jewry contains a bewildering wealth of
statements relating to the tephillin and zizzith. We are told
how long a man should fast if he should drop the tephillin,
and how they are to be cleansed. There are exhaustive discussions as to the proper manner of writing the tephillin; we
learn how large the little box should be, and how long the
thongs, etc. The tephillin were revered almost as much as
the Holy Scriptures.[14] We learn that they, like the Scriptures,
are allowed to be saved from a conflagration on a Sabbath.[15]

In Berak. III, 5, this question is discussed: What is to be
done with the tephillin when the pious Jew goes to the privy?
(It will be remembered that in the time of the Talmud the
tephillin had to be worn all day.) It is recommended that
they should be laid down at a distance of four ells from the
privy; but it is also debated whether or not they should be
held in the hand during evacuation. The possibility of hold-

ing the tephillin in the clothes is rejected, as they might be in danger of falling. It is decided, for example, that it is allowable to take the tephillin into a permanent privy where there is no spray, but not into toilets where there are sprays.

The following story, which is recorded in the Talmud, testifies to the great respect with which tephillin are regarded: it so happened that a youth laid aside his tephillin in an alcove near the street while he went to a toilet. A harlot came by, picked them up, and went into the schoolhouse, saying: "See what that fellow has given me in payment." When the youth heard this he climbed to the summit of the roof, and threw himself down and died.

In the same treatise the problem is debated, between the Rabbis Josefs, Nehunja, and Jehuda, whether one should place the tephillin under one's pillow. It is stated emphatically that they must not be placed under one's feet, since that would be to treat them in a contemptuous manner. Should they be laid between the bolster and the pillow, and would this be allowable if his wife were to lie with the pious Jew, etc.?

The question as to what animal's hide should be employed in preparing the tephillin is answered by referring the matter to Exodus 13, where it is said: "It shall be for a sign . . . that the Lord's law may be in thy mouth"—what you are allowed to take into your mouth: only a ritually clean animal.

That the tephillin must be square was revealed to Moses upon Sinai, and also that they must be wrapped round with the hair of a beast and sewn with its sinews. Even the color of the thongs—which must be black—was revealed to Moses upon Sinai.[16] God himself taught Moses on Sinai how to prepare and bind the tephillin.[17]

It is expressly stated that God himself wears tephillin. This is proved by the passage in Isaiah which says: "The Lord hath sworn by his right hand, and by the arm of his strength." [18] His right hand, according to Deuteronomy means the Law;[19] but his right arm means the tephillin, for it is said: "The Lord will give strength unto his people." [20]

But how—it may be objected—can it be proved that the tephillin are a strength unto Israel? The answer will be found if we refer to Deuteronomy, where we read: "And all the people of the earth shall see that thou art called by the name of the Lord; and they shall be afraid of thee." [21] Rabbi Eliezer the Great explains that what the peoples will be afraid of will be the tephillin of the head. The statement that God Himself wears tephillin is apparently insufficient. The sagacious Rabbi Hijas b. Abin even went so far as to determine what is written in the Lord's tephillin, reciting the precise text contained in each compartment.[22]

From the judgments of the scholars of the Middle Ages we see what importance they attributed to the wearing of the tephillin. Ula, for example, says that if anyone reads the *Sch'ma,* the most important prayer of Jewry, without having put on his tephillin, it is as though he had given false witness against himself.[23] Rabbi Hija b. Abba, on the other hand, compares such behavior to that of a man who has brought a burnt offering without meat or a sacrifice without libation. Rabbi Hija says also: "He who purifies himself and washes his hands and puts on the tephillin and reads the *Sch'ma* and prays, he is accounted by the Scripture as one who has erected an altar and offered up a sacrifice thereon, for it is said: 'I will wash my hands in innocency, sò will I compass thine altar.' " [24] The observance of the injunction as to wearing the tephillin is thus held equal to an offering upon the altar.

Rabbi Schescheth decreed that he who does not wear the tephillin violates eight commandments (since the injunction occurs eight times in the Torah).[25] Rab numbers those who wear no tephillin among the apostates.[26] It is stated emphatically: "So saith the community of Israel: I am chosen from among all the heathen peoples, because I bind the tephillin on the left hand and about the head, and fasten the mezuzah on the right side of my door that the evil spirits may have no power to harm me." [27]

It is a fact that in the Talmud the tephillin, the zizzith, and the mezuzah (the capsules containing biblical verses, fastened to the doorposts), often figure as apotropaic agents, and are usually named together. Maimonides testifies to the sanctifying and protective action of the tephillin; so long as a man has the tephillin on his arm and head he will be humble and God-fearing, and will not turn his thoughts to sin and idleness.[28]

Tephillin, zizzith, and mezuzah, in the Jewish belief, are a protection against sin.[29] This belief was so general that various rabbis surrendered themselves to the most wanton delights, believing themselves to be insured against the danger of sinning because they were equipped with the tephillin. When Abaji (in the third century) was one day seated before Raba and remarked that the latter was behaving in a dissolute manner, he referred him to Psalm 11, where it is written "Rejoice with trembling," but Raba retorted: "I have put on tephillin." [30]

We shall not be surprised to note that the religious opinion of modern Jewry repudiates the belief in the magical character of the tephillin, ascribing to them only an exalted symbolic significance. Thus, according to L. Zunz, though they remind us of things "heavenly" they also warn us against things forbidden: "For if hand and eye are dedicated to God we think with silent reproach of whatsoever impure captures our eye and pollutes our hand." [31]

The connection may seem very vague, but it is stated with great emphasis: "The sign on thy left hand can hold back thy right hand from striking thy brother. The holy memorial that encircles the head fetters the foot when it hastens toward sin." Here, apparently, is no question of a simple defensive mechanism, since from the left hand it reaches the right and from the forehead its influence reaches the intention to transgress. The matter becomes even more complicated and enigmatic, inasmuch as the satchel and thong are supposed to awaken the religious sense of fraternity. We are told: "So often as the symbol is visible on our outward person, so often does the old love bestir itself within, drawing into its hallowed circle all who share our convictions."

Let us now turn to the second object of which the pious Jew must be heedful when he prays, the tassels or fringes which adorn the tallith. The name *zizzith* is related to a root which means "to show forth," so that the word may correctly be translated as "show-threads" (German: *Schaufäden*). Moreover, the scriptural injunction bids the faithful to look upon these threads. The significance and the religious importance of the prescription regarding the zizzith are indicated, not only by the careful exactitude with which it is followed, but also by the repeated expressions in the Talmud, which show what value was attached to the observance of this injunction. The Gemara says: "This commandment is as important as all the commandments in the Torah." [32] "Whoso obeys the commandment regarding the fringes, for him it will be as though he had obeyed all the commandments." [33] In a noteworthy Talmudic interpretation it is said in the passage relating to the fringes, "and ye behold Him [God]"; but not "and ye behold them [the fringes]." This means that he who obeys the injunction relating to the fringes may be said to have received the Lord.[34] Similarly, it is said: "Whosoever is diligent in the observance of this injunction, he beholds God," for it is said "and ye behold Him" (Num. 15:38).[35]

In connection with these statements, individual records are cited which show what importance the zizzith possessed in the eyes of the pious. The son of a famous rabbi was asked what commandment his father had enjoined upon him above all others. He replied: "The law concerning the zizzith. Once, when my father was descending from a ladder he stepped upon one of the threads and tore it, whereupon he refused to move from the spot until the thread was repaired."

Rabbi Resch Lakizeh paints a vivid picture of the rewards which await the pious in the next world. He declares that no fewer than 2800 servants will wait upon every Jew who has observed the injunction concerning the zizzith.[36] For confirmation of this statement he refers to the prophet Zachariah: "In those days it shall come to pass that ten men shall take hold of the skirt of him that is a Jew, saying: We will go with you; for we have heard that God is with you." [37]

The pious man now calculates in the following manner the precise number of servants who in the future would wait upon every Jew: He proceeds from the fact that there are 70 principal languages. He multiplies the number of the lappets of the coat (4) by 10, and so obtains the figure of 2800. It is also related in the Talmud that the zizzith once saved a pious man inasmuch as when he was minded to sin they intervened, as it were, as living witnesses, smiting him in the face "as a reproach." [38]

In this example of a rabbi intimidated by the movement of the zizzith, as in other instances, the fringes figure as a kind of magical instrument. In the course of time this original character became less marked, until they came to be regarded as a symbolic admonition to obey the commandments of God. As an instance of such an anogogic conception of the zizzith I will cite a few sentences from Langfelder's *Die Symbolik des Judentums*.[39] This author emphasizes the fact that the fringes of the Jews "remind them at all hours of the day of the existence of a supreme Judge of the world and Creator: The twisted threads, which have one blue thread in the center, represent a complete symbol of the whole of our human life on earth. On firmly entwined and also innumerable threads the fate of humanity depends on the will of the eternal. . . . The fringes at the four corners of the garment bear witness that the power of God prevails and rules in all four corners of the universe." The fringes in themselves are of course mere threads of white and blue wool. But for the enlightened, for those who have been instructed as to their meaning and their importance, "they comprise a momentous symbol, which represents the relation of mankind to God." Thus the blue thread reminds us "that we are all bound to the heavens, to God, with indissoluble bonds. Because heart and eye inconstantly lust after all earthly joys, and because man is wholly enmeshed and imprisoned by eye and heart, these fringes are so ordered and arranged as to provide and oppose an effective counterpoise to the enticements of the senses."

We may listen indeed to this comprehensive message, but we may yet be unable to believe that the god of a Bedouin tribe can have ordained for his believers so sublime a symbol which would give rise to such trains of thought. The woolen threads are to remind one of human destiny, which is bound up with the will of God. The four corners of the garment typify the four quarters of the universe. The blue thread the infinity of heaven—here is an *embarras de richesse* in symbolic meanings which is surely too momentous even for primitive shepherds who have abundant time for meditation. It is difficult also to imagine why fringes should point to the existence of a supreme Judge of the universe, and what precisely may be the effective counterpoise that is "provided and opposed to the enticements of the senses."

It amazes us to reflect what exalted ethical and religious ideas these threads at the corners of the garment of a nomadic people are supposed to represent. Langfelder, whom I have quoted as the spokesman of modern religious opinion, comes to the following conclusion: "If monotheism has such vitality and viability in Judaism that the 'fringes' can bring the whole order of monotheistic ideas plainly and lucidly to the mind of the beholder, then the rest of the commandments, which convey and represent the same meaning and significance . . . will not be unobserved and disregarded."

If we agree with this conclusion the chances that the rest of God's commandments will be obeyed in the future are somewhat scanty, and the pious man may look toward the days to come with some misgiving, for then the whole order of monotheistic ideas as represented in the "fringes" would no longer be so clear and intelligible as one might wish.

The explanations which the religious and legal traditions of Judaism have to offer us may often sound full of meaning, but they are seldom clear.

III | The theories of Old Testament scholarship and comparative religious criticism

Now consider the representatives of Old Testament scholarship. Though in the literature of Judaism there may be obscure suggestions of the hidden meaning of the prayer thongs and fringes, the sober scholarship of the Hebrew archeologists, which in the last few decades especially has made such great progress through the labors of so many scholars, is certainly better adapted to give us decisive explanations. Here we encounter the cool, transparent atmosphere of rationalism. Here the intellect is supreme, weighing and scrutinizing evidence, and forming its clear judgments. Therefore we may hope for a prompt and reliable solution of the riddle.

As a matter of fact, the critics have long been considering the nature of these mysterious objects. A brief selection of their theories will help to show the direction followed by inquiry, and the nature of the results obtained. If we wish to determine the original significance of the tephillin, our first step should be to discover the etymological meaning of the name of these enigmatic objects. In the Old Testament the designation *totaphot* occurs, a term whose meaning is doubtful. The Talmud calls them tephillin, which may mean head bands or prayer thongs. The Gospels employ the term phylacteries. The Hebrew archeologists were assisted by their knowledge of biblical exegesis, which explains the meaning and the relevance of those passages of the Bible in which there is mention of the tephillin. It was also useful to obtain such data from the experts in comparative religion as it would point to the observance of similar customs among other peoples and in the religious practices of other communities. Talmudic archeology, and exact knowledge of the Jewish liturgy, were called in to assist the work of research.

The still-readable essay on the totaphot which Gottlieb Klein published in 1881[40] finds the derivation of this word in a Hebraic verb meaning to strike or beat. From this the author traces the meaning "lightly touched symbols." According to him, the tephillin were originally a kind of emblem branded upon the forehead. From the context in which the commandment relating to the totaphot first appears, Klein thinks it probable that a bodily mutilation was first indicated by the enigmatic term. The relevant injunctions appear in various passages of the Bible in connection with the Feast of Passover and the Feast of the Firstborn. In Exodus God requires that "all the firstborn shall be sanctified unto me." [41] Thus, the Passover offering of the firstborn, which was made once a year, was no longer sufficient; all the firstborn must bear the sign of dedication to God. This must be the meaning of the Exodus passage: "And it shall be for the sign (ôth) unto thee upon thine hand, and for the memorial (totaphot) between thine eyes." [42]

It is significant that the commandment relating to the totaphot is intimately connected with the dedication of the firstborn at the Feast of Passover. Originally, children were sacrificed physically at this festival. A later age endeavored to obliterate all vestiges of this heathenish method of revering God. The totaphot is, as it were, the last surviving vestige of this sacrifice.

The author or the authors of the other passages in which the totaphot is mentioned were no longer aware of this connection.[43] They no longer understood the original significance of the totaphot as a physical mutilation, conceiving that the injunction was one relating to amulets. According to Klein, we have to distinguish between the original meaning of the totaphot (physical mutilation) and a later meaning (amulets containing verses from the Bible, which originated on Persian soil and under Persian influences). Even the Greek name, phylactery, points to the fact that the totaphot was of the nature of an amulet.

One's first impression of this theory is definitely favorable; more especially because of the context in which the commandment relating to the totaphot first appears. Another point in its favor is that it invokes the genetic standpoint, and is not content with a superficial interpretation of the meaning of the totaphot. It seems probable that there was once a connection, which was no longer recognized at a later period, between the Passover festival and the totaphot.

But it is precisely here that our objections to Klein's ingenious theory have their origins. He claims that the totaphot is derived from the dedication of the firstborn; but later on the law obliged every Jew to dedicate himself to God by special signs upon the hand and between the eyes. But why was every Jew to sanctify the human firstborn? And what was the nature of the connection between that offering and this sign? Why was it to appear on the hand and between the eyes?

The derivation of the word *totaphot* from a verb that means to strike or to beat is more than doubtful. The interpretation of the word as "burned-in symbol" is arbitrary. The totaphot never appears in the Bible or the Talmud as a mutilation; yet there is evidence enough that such religious mutilations did occur. The path leading from these supposed self-mutilations to the institution of the satchels and thongs, which were to be worn constantly, is by no means clear, and is difficult to explain.

The assumption that the misunderstanding of later generations was responsible for this substitution is not a satisfactory explanation. It seems highly probable that the totaphot originally had quite a different significance, now unknown to us, and that it was only at a later period that they came to be regarded as amulets.

The continuity of emotional processes seems to require that this evolution should be such that an inner, psychological connection would exist between the primary, uncomprehended meaning and the subsequent amuletlike character of the totaphot. Also, the shape and structure of the tephillin can hardly, without forcing the idea, be referred back to bodily mutilation. The details of the construction of the satchels and thongs, the particulars of their manufacture, the conspicuous and complicated method of applying them, and the extraordinary opinions held concerning the tephillin can be explained neither by assuming them to signify bodily mutilations nor by regarding them as amulets.

The impression we received on examining Klein's hypothesis is perhaps that of an observer who notes how a wanderer first follows the right path, only quickly to lose it, and ends by going far astray. We feel that a fragment of the desired explanation is contained in the introduction to the theory, but what we were trying to grasp soon escapes us, and leaves us empty-handed.

The explanations furnished by Bernhard Stade constitutes a long step further in the false direction followed by Klein.[44] It is not offered expressly as an attempt to explain the meaning of the tephillin, but it seeks to elucidate the nature of the sign which Jahveh, in the biblical narrative, gave Cain for his protection. Stade tries to establish a connection between this sign of Cain and the wearing of the tephillin. He believes that the sign of Cain was a primitive tattooing. He refers to

Lev. 19:27f., where the Jews are forbidden to "round the corners of the head or mar the corners of the beard"; nor shall they make any cuttings in their flesh for the dead, nor print any marks upon their bodies.

In the Apocalypse the worshipers of the Beast bear the name or number of the Beast on the hand or the forehead.[45] The 144,000 who stand beside the Lamb on the hill of Zion bear the names of the Lamb and his Father written upon their foreheads;[46] they are sealed the servants of God with the name of God upon their foreheads.[47] One of the relics of such an ancient sign of Jahveh, almost effaced by the hand of an editor, will be found in the passage of Exodus in which the "law of the totaphot" appears.[48] It is evident that the object mentioned is a cultic memorial emblem; that is, a sign which reminds the wearer of his membership in a cult. The passages in Deuteronomy (X1, 8 and V1, 8) express the obligation to bear the commandments of God in memory ("in their heart"), in the plastic form. They are to be bound upon the hand and worn as totaphot between the eyes.

The choice of the expression *bind* indicates that here the plastic image is employed in a secondary sense, since what is bound on is detachable. This choice of words represents the attempt at a later material interpretation. By this the step was already taken which in Judaism led to the invention of the Talmudic tephillin, the Judaeo-Hellenic phylacteries.

The ancient custom of tattooing, which was afterward felt to be heathenish was now eradicated by the innovation: "The sign scratched or burned into the body, since it had become repugnant in a religious sense, will have been replaced by a substitute which was no longer repugnant." [49] The law intervened, taking the place of the old heathen magic, as it has often done in the Christian church also. The old cultic importance of the Jewish tephillin is revealed only by the fact that "these articles of clothing, inherently difficult of explanation," were worn during religious worship. The "mark

of Cain" is identical with, or related to, the Israelite totaphot.—One must admit that this aspect of Stade's theory
represents an advance upon the earlier views, since it emphasizes the character of the totaphot as a cultic emblem.
What there is to be said against it was said in our discussion
of Klein's opinion. We felt that it was advanced by an inquirer who has not made a sufficient endeavor to find a basis
for his views. It does not explain how a system of satchels and
thongs could develop from the practice of tattooing, and it
throws no light on the special importance in Judaism or on
the peculiar ritual of the tephillin.

Baentsch likewise believes that the totaphot are to be regarded as amulets.[50] The practice of wearing amulets on the
forehead is only a modification of an older practice—that of
cutting or scratching a Jahveh sign on the forehead. The old
sign was intended to remind the wearer of his cultic obliga-
tions. The passage in Exodus (13:16) signifies that the offering of the firstborn was to be such a token of remembrance
and admonition. It reminds Israel that Jahveh once smote
the firstborn of the Egyptians.

Like Stade, Baentsch comes to the conclusion that the literal understanding or misunderstanding of this passage or
of other parallel passages, led later on to the invention of the
tephillin or phylacteries. The development was therefore as
follows: An ancient tattooed cultic emblem—an amulet—
the invention of the tephillin.

Holzinger also thinks of a tattooed Jahveh sign.[51] Wellhausen considers that the totaphot were amulets fastened
upon headbands.[52] According to W. Robertson Smith the
phylacteries are survivals of ancient superstition, and their
employment during prayer may indicate the nature of this
superstition.[53] They are appliances for the purpose of increasing the efficacy of prayer.

The belief that the totaphot are amulets is supported also
by Grünbaum,[54] Blau[55] (who refers to the scarabs of the

Egyptian priests), and Bousset [56] ("If the New Testament calls them amulets the original significance of this custom is correctly indicated. . . . The prayer capsules will have suppressed the original practice of bearing tattooed emblems of Jahveh on forehead and arm"). Similar opinions are held by Schürer[57] (the Greek designation shows that the chief importance of the tephillin lay in the fact that they "kept evil spirits at a distance during prayer"), Wünsche,[58] Kittel,[59] Nowak,[60] and many other scholars.

It became more and more obvious that the progressive representatives of religious research believed that they had solved the problem by resorting to the designation of phylacteries and regarding the tephillin as amulets. Here again the scholars have, on the whole, obeyed wise advice to rely on words.

Only rarely does there emerge a timid doubt as to whether this can be the real meaning of the tephillin. Such doubts were unwelcome, and were quickly dispelled by the calm certainty of traditional learning. Thus Friedländer's argument proceeded from a curious passage in the Mischna: "Whosoever bears the tephillin on the forehead or on the palms of the hands; he is following the custom of the Minaeans [heretics]." [61]

Friedländer sees the explanation of this enigmatic decision in the fact that the Minaeans used to wear certain cultic emblems which the rabbis endeavored to supplant with the tephillin. For example, they were substituted for the snake-mark (*signum serpentinum*) of the pre-Christian Gnostics. The rabbis sought to obliterate every trace of such heretical symbols. In support of his opinion that the tephillin were not a genuinely Jewish creation, but were employed to suppress the Gnostic *signum serpentinum*, Friedländer referred to the many indications of uncertainty in the Talmudic discussion of the tephillin; for example, the debate as to whether they should be worn on the right hand or the left, and the hesitation to regard them as directly commanded by the Torah, and so on.

According to Friedländer, the course of development would have been more or less as follows: Gnostic signs introduced themselves into the broad masses of the Jewish people. Then, since they could no longer be suppressed, "they were sanctioned, having been first given a Mosaic garment." [62] It was easily shown that this hypothesis of Friedländer's was untenable. The religious practice of wearing tephillin dates back to a time far earlier than that of the Jewish Gnostics. Still, despite the justifiable rejection of Friedländer's theory, one could not refuse to recognize the spark of truth contained among so many errors.

The question over which the scholars are still debating is whether the biblical passages in which the injunction regarding the totaphot appears are to be accepted literally or metaphysically. Emil G. Hirsch, for example, begins by stating that those four passages in the Bible seem to prove that the custom of wearing amuletlike objects on the hand and the forehead was very widespread.[63] The later rabbinical exegesis has taken the simile contained in these passages literally, and has proceeded in accordance with the literal meaning.

Edward Mack inclines to the opinion that in these biblical verses there is an allusion to visible jewels or amulets, such as were worn by the neighboring heathen tribes, and that this allusion is a poetical comparison.[64] A careful reading of the passages in question yields proof of their purely metaphorical significance. The ceremonial of the tephillin represents a degradation of an idealistic figure of speech occurring in the Old Testament. "Only the formalism of later periods could interpret this metaphor in the crude and materialistic practice of wearing phylacteries."

A. R. S. Kennedy, too, after an exhaustive examination of the passages in question, comes to the conclusion "that the languages of these verses is purely symbolical." [65]

Kennedy, with reference to "the sign upon thine hand," points to the general practice of tattooing among primitive peoples. The forehead also is a favorite place for such tattooed symbols among half-savage tribes. We find that Kennedy returns to Stade's theory, and confirms it, inasmuch as he cites other passages of the Bible he regards as evidence of such practice: the young man who bore a sign upon his forehead which showed that he was a prophet; the cross mentioned by Ezekiel, and "the sign of destruction" on the forehead of the wicked.

The scholars have debated the meaning of the word *totaphot* used in biblical passages[66] for the token Jahveh requires to be worn on the arm and the forehead. Knobel derives the word from a root which means "to strike" and then "to make an incision." Thus, totaphot would signify a tattoo mark or a branded mark. Klein, Siegfried, Stade, Nowak, and many other scholars support this opinion. On the other hand, König and other scholars have agreed that the word comes from a root related to the Arabic *tâfa* (to encircle), and has been produced by reduplication. From this, as Gesenius, Dillman, Driver, and others maintain, is derived the meaning "that which goes round the forehead"—a headband. Steuernagel also proposes the meaning, "an encircling band."

If the derivation from the Arabic word *tâfa* is correct, then the interpretation of the word as headband is not consistent with the explicit location "between thine eyes." Kennedy, moreover, stresses the point that such an interpretation is not compatible with the group of ideas from which the metaphor is taken. Yielding to the force of this argument, recent research has again rejected the derivation from *tâfa*. In the absence of any other reasonable interpretation, Kennedy refers to a root which means to drop or to drip. It then belongs to the order of designations for the apotropaic jewels which were worn in Israel.

The author of Deuteronomy did not hesitate to employ so

crude a metaphor in order to express the notion that the commandments of Yahweh should always be as close to the thoughts of the people and as highly treasured as were the most precious jewels among their superstitious contemporaries.[67]

As a curiosity, it may be noted that König has found the derivation of the word *totaphot* from another Arabic root, which points to the meaning "field of vision." In line with this interpretation, König translates Deut. 11:8 as follows "All the more shall ye lay up these words in your heart and your soul and bind them as a sign of remembrance on your hand and let them be as a field of vision between your eyes." This version is not lacking in elegance, but it may arouse a slight doubt as to whether the scholar has completely grasped the spirit of this passage.

The other problem—the date when the wearing of the tephillin was introduced—is closely connected with the question that has just been discussed. If we are dealing, as the majority of the scholars believe, with a novel institution, which was based on the misunderstanding of a biblical text, it should be possible, through research into the existing sources, to determine approximately the date of this new religious practice.

The Talmud, of course, assures us that the wearing of the tephillin was in accordance with instructions given to Moses by God on Sinai. Wünsche attributes the introduction of the totaphot to the pre-Christian era.[68] Klein believes that it originated on Persian soil.[69] Buhl suggests a hypothetical date on the grounds that "the later use of the totaphot or tephillin, evoked by a more comprehensive grasp of the passages in question, cannot be proved in the Old Testament scriptures." [70] This is true, but what is adduced as proof has itself to be proven.

The question which is here represented as settled by an incidental attribute is the question whether such a later and more comprehensive grasp of the relevant passages was a reality. Kennedy asks himself in what period of Jewish history those four passages were first interpreted literally.[71] If we compare similar turns of speech employed in aphorisms with these, we arrive at the year 300 B.C. as approximately the *terminus a quo*. The *terminus ad quem* appears to be given by the famous letter of the pseudo Aristeas, in which it is stated that Eleazar taught that Moses commanded us, in addition to affixing tokens of remembrance on our clothing, and verses to doorposts and gateposts, also to fasten signs upon the hand.

Here, then, is an unmistakable reference to the hand tephillah. In this way Kennedy arrives at a period extending from 250 to 150 B.C.[72] On general and psychological grounds, moreover, it seems probable that this period saw the introduction of phylacteries, since it was marked by the rise of the ritualistic fanaticism which attributed the greatest importance to literal obedience to the Torah. During this period the Pharisees acquired great influence over the people and enforced their rigorous opinions in matters of ritual. It is probable that the religious practice of wearing the tephillin was among the observances enjoined upon the people.[73] Josephus regarded the wearing of the tephillin as an ancient practice. His contemporaries were of the same opinion.[74]

If we have no definite information as to when the custom of wearing the tephillin originated in Jewry, the pronouncements of the Mishna give us abundant information relating to the period after the birth of Christ. We have already mentioned most of these disputations, prescriptions, and questions. During the Middle Ages, the great mass of people seem often to have wavered in their obedience to this particular law. At all events, in the eighth century, and more particularly in the tenth, the tephillin were less highly regarded; indeed in many regions the religious practice had almost entirely lapsed.[75] It seems as though the faithful reverted to it with increased zeal after the many attacks from the advocates of reforms.

The religious ceremonial of wearing the zizzith has been discussed by the scholars no less exhaustively than has the wearing of the tephillin. But in this case the agreement has been general that the practice is of great antiquity. As we see on the monuments of Persepolis, similar tassels or "fringes" were worn on the corners of the garments of the ancient Persians. Thureau-Daugin has shown that in the time of the first Babylonian dynasty the impression "of the fringed border of a man's mantle" served as a seal or signature.[76] The representations of Syrian and other Asiatic peoples on ancient Egyptian monuments furnish evidence that this kind of ornament was habitually worn by the tribes neighboring Israel.[77] Kennedy points out that the position of the "fringes" on the four corners of the garment is connected with certain superstitious notions which have left their traces in Hebraic legislation. He mentions, as an example, the bells on the official robe of the high priest,[78] which McNeil has explained in a similar sense.[79] Kennedy comes to the conclusion that the tassels were originally amulets.

Baentsch also thinks that the wearing of such tassels may "somehow" be referred to an ancient custom; the people of a later age, who no longer understood the meaning of the practice, evolved the explanation which appears in the Israelite law. At all events, the tassels or fringes, like the tephillin, had originally the significance of phylacteries or amulets.[80] König thinks it obvious that the notion of Israel's special relationship to Deity was to be symbolized by the attachment of tassels to the blankets of Israel. This scholar, however, whose originality we have already acknowledged, is remarkably backward in explaining how the addition of tassels to blankets is supposed to symbolize "the special relationship of Israel to the Deity."

However, other scholars who have interested themselves in this detail of Hebraic archeology have observed that originally the zizzith had doubtless the character of amulets. In this connection we should give special attention to W. Robertson Smith's reminder that among the ancient Semites the hide of certain animals was sacred, and that its use had originally a religious significance. Smith suggests that the fringes prescribed by the Jewish law are more or less distantly related to the *raht* or *hauf*, an Arabian girdle or short fur tunic, such as was worn by maidens during menstruation and by the faithful before the Kaaba. With these one may compare the thongs of the Luperci in ancient Rome, which were cut from the hide of sacrificial animals.

This theory, which W. Robertson Smith incidentally advances in a footnote, seems to me to come nearer to an understanding of the mysterious tassels than the other attempts at explanation on the part of the Old Testament and Near Eastern experts. Here we find a fresh point of view which the other scholars did not and do not now take into consideration. For the first time attention is given to the material from which these mysterious fringes were prepared. The sacredness of the hide of certain animals acquires a special significance under this hypothesis. We may anticipate that the prosecution of Smith's theory will lead to definite conclusions as to the meaning of this custom.

Such research seems all the more necessary if we wish to learn why such an important role was ascribed to tassels or fringes in particular, what their original meaning and function can have been, how they acquired the character of amulets, and how the complicated Talmudic prescriptions are to be explained. Smith, in this hypothesis, has achieved more than all the efforts of the archeologists and biblical critics. It is definitely important, for it is highly suggestive; but the explanations it has afforded so far have been too general to solve the enigma of the zizzith.

I V | Exegesis and the criticism of sources

We must once more return to the four biblical passages in
which the prescriptions for wearing the tephillin are contained. Exodus 13:9 forms part of a chapter which contains
the commandments relating to the feast of the Mazzoth and
the offering of the firstborn. Here, suddenly—apparently
without transition—appears the commandment: "And it
shall be for a sign [ôth] unto thee upon thine hand and for a
memorial [zikkaron] between thine eyes that the Lord's law
may be in thy mouth; for with a strong hand hath the Lord
brought thee out of Egypt." [81]

The passage is very obscure. Dillman and Kautsch assume that the text is imperfect. The question naturally arises
as to what such a sign would be. The text says it. Immediately before this is the commandment to eat unleavened
bread for seven days. Baentsch straightway assumes that the
enigmatical "it" relates to this custom.[82] Holzinger, on the
other hand, considers that the sentence is overloaded; the
subject is not clearly indicated.[83] Baentsch would interpret
the verse thus: "Israel is to keep the Torah of Israel in its
mouth; that is, diligently meditate upon it and make it the
subject of instructive and improving speech."

But this cannot possibly be the original meaning of the
passage, for, according to the context, the Torah does not
yet exist. It will be given to Israel only very much later. Can
the it relate to the offering of the firstborn, which is mentioned in the succeeding passage? But what could be meant
by the statement that it shall be "for a sign unto thee upon
thine hand" and "a memorial between thine eyes"?

The injunction is repeated in Exodus 13:16. There
(13:14) we read: "And it shall be when thy son asketh thee

in time to come, saying, What is this? that thou shalt say unto him, By strength of hand the Lord slew all the first-born in the land of Egypt, both the firstborn of man and the firstborn of beast; therefore I sacrificed to the Lord all that openeth the matrix, being males; but all the firstborn of my children I redeem." Now, almost unaltered, follows the com-mandment: "And it shall be for a token upon thine hand, and for frontlets between thine eyes," etc.

Baentsch observes at this point: "This custom also is to serve as a memorial," though it is difficult to see what con-nection there can be between the sacrifice of the firstborn and the sign upon the hand and between the eyes. Kennedy is of much the same opinion as Baentsch: the feast of the Maz-zoth, like the sacrifice of the firstborn, is to serve as a per-petual memorial of the liberation of the Hebrews from the Egyptian captivity and of the Lord's requirement of them.[84]

The context of the third passage, Deuteronomy 6:6ff., is as follows: "Hear, O Israel: The Lord our God is one Lord. And thou shalt love the Lord thy God with all thine heart and with all thy soul and with all thy might." According to Bertholet this paranetic introductory speech is characterized by "its own urgent warmth of tone." "The speaker addresses himself *ad hominem* and expressly emphasizes the intimate relation of the human being to God." [85] The continuation of this appeal, which has resulted in its being recited, morning and evening, by every adult Jew as a confession (*sch'ma*), is as follows: "And these words which I command thee this day shall be in thine heart; and thou shalt teach them diligently unto thy children, and shall talk of them when thou sittest in thine house, and when thou walkest by the way, and when thou liest down, and when thou risest up. And thou shalt bind them for a sign upon thine hand and have them as totaphot between thine eyes," etc.

Steuernagel observes that the relative clause, "which I command thee this day," seems to postulate their relation to the Law. He proposes to omit the clause, since "a reference to the law in this form before its communication would not be really intelligible." [86] In Steuernagel's opinion we have in this relative clause one of the favorite conventional additions of the transcriber, who was always thinking only of the Law. In Deuteronomy (11:18-20) the commandment appears again in almost the same words. The biblical scholars consider that in this passage there is a quotation from Deuteronomy 6:6-9. We have apparently a late version, since the text of the first passage is not completely reproduced.

These two passages in Deuteronomy are, in Kennedy's opinion, "the cardinal passages" on which the ancient Jewish usage of the phylacteries is based.[87] "We have to ask ourselves, do these passages command and sanction the religious usage or do they not command it? To answer this is by no means as easy as may appear at first sight, for it is not only a matter of exegesis, but it involves the consideration of problems of biblical criticism and etymological research." Kennedy, returning to the hypothesis already mentioned, suggests that the author or rather the authors of these passages have here employed a metaphor, and interprets the word *totaphot* as "drops" or "jewels."

Other Old Testament scholars have carefully examined the text of these four passages to which the institution of the tephillin is attributed. They have striven, with extraordinary care, to identify the various sources of these verses, and to place them in the known religious and historical context of Israel's development.

If we summarize the views of the scholars regarding these important passages, we find a consensus that they are to be accepted metaphorically. It may well be—so many of them consider—that the editors of the Bible have made use of a comparison which is based upon the practice of an ancient national custom, a tattoo or a Jahveh sign. No doubt we are dealing with a figure of speech.

Be this as it may, it seems to me that we may usefully note a few characteristics which these four passages appear to have in common. The law, or whatever the *it* may signify, is to be for Israel as an *ôth*—a sign, *signum,* on the hand, and as zik-karon or totaphot between the eyes. We know neither what this sign is to be nor its nature, since according to the experts we have to regard the invention of the tephillin as a later institution, based upon a misunderstanding of the text.

It is, however, undeniable that here the reference is to a sign or memorial. Further, we note that in all four passages there is the recommendation to teach *them* to the children, to "talk of them."

One other common feature may be mentioned—the circumstances under which the commandment is uttered. It is somehow connected with the Feast of Passover. The firstborn, the sacrifice of the firstlings, have something to do with this mysterious memorial sign. In three passages this sign is designated by the word *totaphot.* The meaning of this word is obscure. The Greek translation is *asaleuton,* something immovable; the Vulgate says *appensum quid,* something attached. In any case, the word is used in the same sense as *ôth* and *zikkaron,* and subsequently it acquired the meaning of sign or commemorative sign. For the moment, I incline to the opinion that the root of the word originally meant to go about, to circumscribe.

We now find ourselves in a curious situation. On the one hand, religious tradition tells us that the tephillin are memorial signs; that God commanded the Jews to use them, speaking to Moses on Sinai; and that they are of the greatest religious importance. We do not know, indeed, of what they are supposed to remind the bearer. We do not believe that Moses received a revelation from God and we do not understand why such importance should be ascribed to a combination of satchels and thongs.

Old Testament scholarship asserts, in opposition to religious tradition, that we are dealing with a late invention, which has no connection with the original Israelite religion. A biblical text which should have been understood in a meta-phorical sense was understood literally and misunderstood, many centuries later. From this misunderstanding the insti-tution of the tephillin originated. They were amulets, in-tended to keep evil spirits at a distance.

The ancient, traditional view seems wholly absurd. At all events, as regards its connection with the religious use of the tephillin it is unintelligible. A literal understanding of the biblical passages appears at first sight to make sheer nonsense. The explanations of the biblical archeologists cannot eliminate all contradictions. There remain, so to speak, errors of weav-ing in the carpet which they offer us, but it seems reasonable and consistent with our way of thinking. Thus, the choice before us is not a difficult one, if we accept the rational solu-tion. It must be confessed, however, that there is a trifling obstacle in the way of whole-hearted acceptance. Here is just one of those curious contradictions which the rational ap-proach is unable to solve.

v | Another attempt at explanation

In a situation of this kind psychoanalysis again seems to me particularly appropriate. We remember the judgments the strict theologians have passed on the achievements of analy-sis, insofar as they relate to religion and religious problems. In particular, they reproach the psychoanalysts with introduc-ing hypotheses which cannot be proved, or do not appear to have been proven. The critics say that the analysts apply without any justification results obtained in the alien sphere of the psychology of the neuroses to the investigation of reli-gious problems. We psychoanalysts cannot regard these reproaches as a reason for discontinuing our work in the theological field. We even feel that in this field we are pioneers, and that we can wait until the theologians recognize what a rich and fruitful region we have conquered for them to investigate.

Here, by exception and only in this special case, a concession may be made in order to satisfy the requirements of the theological discipline. In the following attempt to divine the original meaning of the tephillin and zizzith, not a single analytical hypothesis arising from the psychology of the neuroses has been applied. None of the results obtained by such analytic treatment have been adduced. Here psychoanalysis is applied only as a heuristic method. As such it should prove whether it is possible to solve a special problem of theological science without hypotheses—one of those numerous problems which this science is unable to solve by its own methods. On the basis of small and hitherto unregarded individual features, psychoanalysis yields results in connection with this problem which even the representatives of the alien science will be obliged to accept—surprising and unfamiliar though they may at the first glance appear. We are not, however, especially interested in this result. What we should wish is to see the psychoanalytic method applied in its purest form to the work of research. And this is precisely where the methods hitherto applied by theological science could result only in flagrant failure.

An old book which came into my hands by chance may serve as the starting point of our analytical investigation. It is entitled *Die Alten Jüdischen Heiligtümer/Gottes-Dienste und Gewohnheiten/für Augen gestellet/in einer ausführlichen Beschreibung des gantzen Levitischen Priestertums/ und fünf unterschiedenen Büchern* etc., Hamburg 1701.[88] Its author was Johannes Lund, represented on the title page as a faithful servant of the Word of God at Tundern in the Duchy of Schleswig. This old book gives a faithful description of the religious institutions of the Israelites in antiquity and in the author's own time, in clear and vigorous German.

One section is devoted to the tephillin. The "faithful servant of God's word" describes exactly these particular religious objects as they lay before him. Of the strips of parchment inscribed with biblical verses which are contained in the tephillin he says: "These are wound about with the hair of cows or calves/which are pulled out of their tails/ and previously well washed and purified. These hairs, however, are not knotted at the end/but only twisted round with the fingers/so as to allow one hair/to stand out/so that it is seen from without. . . ." [89]

Now, we already know that these parchments are tied with the hair of a ritually clean animal. It may well be that the end of a hair protruded from the capsule. As a matter of fact, in the tephillin of orthodox Jews we still find that the hair with which the parchment is tied protrudes a little way from the capsule. But after all, how does this bit of hair concern us? It may or may not protrude a little from the head tephillah; surely this detail is meaningless?

Nonetheless, let us read on and see what the faithful Johannes Lund has to tell us concerning this usage. He is not content to examine and describe exactly the religious objects before him; he has made exhaustive inquiries of the authorities of his day as to their details. He tells us of an interview he had about this very usage with a rabbi of Amsterdam. First of all, he informs us that he observed this peculiar hair in the case of this rabbi's tephillah: "A red hair was hanging out of it/almost as long/as one and a half joints of the finger. I inquired as to the reason of this. He said/it would be in remembrance of the red cow/and that they prayed to God/that/as the red cow had taken their sins upon her/and cleansed them of their impurities/God would also cleanse them of their sins/Novarin Schediasn, book 5, chap. 28 writes/he too had questioned a Jew as to this/and received the answer/that they were reminded thereby of the golden calf/which they had worshipped in the wilderness." [90]

Now, here is a detail which is quite unimportant even for those who are interested in the evolution of religious beliefs. We are certainly not impressed by the statement that the Jews connect this little bit of hair protruding from the head tephillah with the red cow or the golden calf. How should such a detail, such a trifle as an inch of hair, set us on the track of the original significance of the tephillin?

The analytic method insists that just such unregarded details are of the greatest heuristic value. Another of its methodical principles is to take the hints furnished by tradition seriously in a psychological sense, however foolish or meaningless they may seem. We follow the methodical hint it gives us: What can it signify that this tip of a hair should remind pious Jews of the red cow or of the calf that their ancestors once worshiped in the wilderness? What heuristic value can attach to such a mystical or seemingly absurd statement?

If the head tephillah is to be applied to the forehead near the edge of the scalp, and if the hair of a cow or a calf protrudes from it, and further, if the Jews assert that this hair is to remind them of the red cow, or of this calf on Sinai—is there not a suggestion that the head tephillah itself is an article of clothing or a disguise which represents the wearer symbolically as a bull, or—in more general parlance—as an ox? The material of which the head tephillah is made is in no way inconsistent with such an assumption. The Law itself requires that it be made of the hide of an ox. Even its form supports the theory; for we have here a relic, a suggestion, of the horns of the beast, which jut forward from its head.

The hypothesis at which we should arrive by following this line of thought, fantastic though it may seem at first sight, would be this: The head tephillah is a relic, a survival, of a disguise which the Israelites adopted on certain occasions.

From this point of view it would not be difficult to offer an explanation of the meaning of the hand tephillah and the thongs, or of the tallith and the zizzith. We should conclude that these articles of clothing also represent some such primitive fashion of disguise. The hand tephillah might represent the hoof of the ox; the leather thongs, as *pars pro toto,* would represent its hide.

And even the tallith, made from the wool of a ritually clean animal, might be the substitute for the fleece of a ram, originally roughly cured and worn by the Hebraic tribes. The zizzith would then be allusions to the animal's four legs, and the knotting of the many threads would represent the joints. We should thus have uncovered the traces of ancient tribal custom, from which the original meaning of the tephillin and the zizzith is derived.

In the arms of the city of Danzig are the words *"Nec timide nec temere."* Let them serve as the motto of this inquiry. The analytic method has led us, through the psychological consideration of this detail, to a seemingly fantastic assumption concerning the meaning of the phylacteries. If we wish in all seriousness to maintain our allegation, it is incumbent upon us to establish its probability. First we must deal with all the objections which our hypothesis is bound to provoke, disregarding all the contradictions it seems to contain. We ask ourselves: What could be the meaning of such an animal disguise? What could be the motive of such a device?

VI | The living raiment of God

Comparative ethnology tells us that the majority of primitive and semiprimitive tribes employ such disguises for purposes of magic. The belief that by putting on the hide of an animal one becomes that animal is general among primitive peoples. Frazer describes how the savage wraps himself in the skin of a totemic animal, or fastens upon his person certain parts of the animal's pelt, in order to make sure of the totem's protection. Certain Indian tribes wrap themselves in the skins of wolves. A hole is made in the skin, through which the head of the man protrudes, while the head of the wolf hangs on the warrior's breast.[91] Lewis and Clarke reported that on certain occasions the Teton Indians wear a raven on the head, the body being divided, one half coming down on either side of the human head.[92] Most of the Indian tribesmen appear on solemn occasions, as at feasts or dances, in such animal disguises, and as a rule every tribesman wears at least a recognizable portion of a totemic animal on his person. For example, the Condor Indians in Peru wear on their heads the feathers of this bird, from which they trace their descent. The warriors of the Buffalo Indians arrange two locks of their hair in such a way as to imitate the horns of the buffalo. Many Australian tribes cut thongs from the hide of certain animals and fasten them all over their bodies, in order to resemble the animals.

The peoples of antiquity held the same views concerning the special significance of an animal's hide or pelt. W. R. Smith tells us that among the Semitic tribes in ancient times the hide of the sacrificial animal possessed a character of special sanctity. It was employed in the ancient religions to clothe either the image of the god or his worshipers.[93]

The significance of this custom was obvious in a phase of religious evolution in which the god, his worshipers, and the sacrificial victim were all members of the same tribe. Smith argues that the worshiper of the god who clothes himself in the skin of a sacrificed animal thereby invests himself with the sanctity of the animal so that for half-savage peoples clothes are a permanent factor of the social religion, a token of membership of the religion. Herodotus tells us that the *aegis,* the goatskin, was a sacred garment among the Libyans.

Smith compares the tassels or fringes on the garment, prescribed by Jewish law, with the thongs of the sacred goatskin. He likewise observes that at a later period the hide of the sacrificed animal always played an important part in connection with religious usages and especially in the ceremonials of atonement. The Assyrian worshipers of Dagon, who make the mystical fish sacrifice to the fish-god, wrap themselves in the skin of a fish. When a sacrifice was offered to the sheep-goddess of Cyprus, the worshiper wrapped himself in a sheepskin. In Hierapolis the pilgrim placed the head and feet of the sacrifice on his own head, while he knelt on the skin. In certain late Syrian cults a boy received religious lustration through a sacrifice, his feet being shod with shoes made from the skin of the sacrificial animal. Even in the later forms of religion the old usages persist, at all events in the religious employment of animal masks. In almost every crude religion there are related features. They are to be found also in the Dionysian mysteries and other Greek rites.

We think we can guess now what motives led the ancient Israelites to disguise themselves with animal skins or parts of an animal. They were the same motives as those that actuated the Semitic people of antiquity, and which actuate the primitive peoples of the present day. They bestow on these animal disguises a special religious and social significance.

We may assume then that originally the Hebraic tribes clad themselves in the skins of their totemic animal, whether this was the bull or the ram.[94] They identified themselves with the sacred animal so completely that they regarded it as their tribal ancestor and protector. This was their way—and the way of all ancient people—of showing that they were proud of the blood relationship with the animal, and of partaking of its qualities.

We must naturally imagine that originally it was almost the entire hide in which the ancient Hebrews wrapped themselves. With the decline of primitive totemism, and un-

der the influence of various other motives, many changes occurred in this religious custom. There cannot have been only
social reasons which forbade the Hebrews to wear the old
tribal tokens proudly and openly. The totemic religion itself
gradually lost its importance. As among other half-savage
tribes, at a later period only individual parts of the animal's
skin were employed to indicate an identification with the totemic animal, and to place the wearer under its protection.

What was once of the greatest importance now seems reduced to the extreme in its dimensions. What was formerly
of the greatest significance is now merely indicated and transferred to the merest detail. In the place of natural members
of the animal (perhaps the horns of the bull) artificial substitute devices, allusions to the originals, must have made
their appearance. Their connection with the ancient token
consists only in the identity of their material and their similarity in shape. Their special sanctity, and their employment
in ritual and cultic exercise, were indicated by the fact that
they had to continue the ancient function.

From the position which we have now reached it should
not be difficult to define the difference between our views
and those of our predecessors. These Old Testament scholars
were mostly of the opinion that the totaphot were originally
either bodily mutilations or amulets. This cannot be the case,
though the tephillin might subsequently have acquired the
character of amulets, just as every portion of a totemic animal can assume the function of protection, and often does,
there is no evidence to connect the totaphot with bodily mutilations.

Nevertheless, this hypothesis leads us toward the actual
origin of the tephillin. The tattooings or bodily markings are
attempts at assimilation to or identification with the totem
of the primitive tribe. Those investigators who assume that
the totaphot were originally Jahveh signs or natural emblems
were on the right track. They cannot tell us, however, what

was the nature of the sign, what function it had, and why it took this particular form. One might say that most of the representatives of Old Testament archeology had individual fragments of the great complex in their hands, but that the factual and psychological connection between these elements was wholly lacking. We have to thank psychoanalysis for a hypothesis which can supply the "missing link." The tephillin are a substitute for those portions of the totemic pelt the ancient Israelites wore in order to identify themselves with their totemic god.

From this it becomes evident how erroneous is the opinion held by the majority of archeologists—that the institution of the tephillin was an invention of the late rabbinical Judaism, having originated about a century before the birth of Christ. Of this there can be no question. Our views concerning the original significance and function of the totaphot refers the origins of the tephillin to the prehistoric age of the Hebrew tribe, when totemism was still a living memory.

When, later on, the worship of Jahveh suppressed the old totemistic ideas, these latter were not eliminated. A process of new interpretation and amalgamation of the two orders of religious ideas occurred. For a long while the new religion of Yahveh, fighting for its existence, made use of the old totemistic forms, and indeed never entirely superseded them. Subterraneously, and in new psychological connections, not perceived consciously, the ancient totemic cult forced its way through the laws of the new faith, and the inherited notions spread rapidly over the now-enforced ideology, to which the conservatism and stubborn tenacity of the Hebraic tribes refused for a long while to adapt themselves.

While at a later period the tephillin may have assumed the indifferent character of religious amulets, everything goes to indicate that they were once the substitutes for the sacred animal pelt, the living garment of the god. Their function, within the framework of an "enlightened" Judaism and a tepid rationalism, may have been merely accessory and purely symbolical. Analytic investigation, however, is able to show that the unbroken, unconscious thought association of the pious with the emotional and intellectual life of their ancestors comes closer to the mystery than the rigid *akribia* and seeming objectivity of a science which approaches the unconscious without preconceived opinions.

Psychoanalysis is able to give us profounder conclusions concerning the apparently unimportant detail of the tephillin than theology, which can do no more here than recognize some sort of indifferent cultic signs, or the relics of incised emblems. Our inquiry seems to result in the admonition *Introite, et hic dii sunt.*

VII | Objections, corrections, and addenda

It is true that many problems remain to be solved, but now it is time to deal with the objections we have for so long disregarded. The most important of these is based on the fact that our theory contains inherent contradictions that endanger its validity. For example, we have assumed that the tallith is a relic of a representation of the sacred ram's fleece. The zizzith would then represent the four legs of the animal. The arrangement of threads and knots we have observed represents, by allusion, the muscles and joints of the sacred animal. Here, of course, it may be objected that these threads, in their arrangement, can hardly be compared with the feet of an animal, but the brevity of the tallith belongs to a later stage of development. Originally it was a long garment. Lund tells us that the tallith "were so long that not a hand's breadth of the undergarment could be seen beneath them. The fringes had to hang to the ground in such a manner that the above-mentioned Rabbi Jacob Abraham and also Christian

Gottlieb assured me that in Poland many rabbis wore their Arba Canpos or the Jewish dress with fringes so long that the latter reached the ground and often trailed after them." [95]

The abbreviation of these combinations of threads, which were at first worn long, had thus resulted in making their original signification unrecognizable. A similar reduction of certain features of religious usages under the influence of cultural changes has often resulted in obscuring the primary significance of a cult or of many of its rites. Often enough another secondary meaning is given precedence over the old meaning which has already become unintelligible.

When the original significance of a rite or custom has been discovered by research, a psychological analysis should succeed in showing that numerous connections exist between the secondary and the primary meaning. The change of meaning may be said to follow a prescribed path. Thus the tephillah, which was originally a portion of the divinity himself, became an amulet. This means that he who wears such a fragment of the god upon his person, or carries it with him, is under the special protection of the god.

Such a significance is naturally a derived one. Originally the wearer of the tephillin became the god himself, and gods have no need of amulets. Even in the later, artificially established associations the original meaning still glimmers through the apparently uninterrupted context, as the first text of a palimpsest may often be deciphered between the letters of the later script. Do we not recognize it when religious tradition declares that the thongs of the head tephillah form, in their convolutions, the letters of God's name? Here the original meaning of the tephillin glimmers through the latest interpretation. The prehistoric totemistic god of an age which certainly knew nothing of letters reappears in this indirect manner in the curiously formed letters.

Can we not recognize the original character of the zizzith in the mystical allusions to their numerical value? Do they

not now say that "the Lord is one," and now give the numbers of the religious commandments? But the essential law
of the primitive religion is really this identification of the believer with his god, whose garment he wears. The Lord himself wore tephillin—for confirmation, think of the original
significance of the horns which adorn the sacred animal.

The Talmud explains the biblical prophecy according to
which the peoples of the earth were to be afraid before Israel
by stating that the nations were to be afraid before the head
tephillah. Can we not here detect an allusion to the original
meaning of the national totem, worn on the head? The other
Talmudic interpretation, which explains the passage "ye behold him" (not "ye behold them"—the fringes) is akin to
the former. What it really says is: He who beholds the zizzith
sees God, and this is true in the sense of *pars pro toto,* for
the zizzith are the substitute for a fragment of the divinity;
they represent themselves. In the Talmud the wearing of
the zizzith is equivalent to obeying all the commandments of
the ceremonial religion. Psychologically this is correct: The
identification with the ancient totemic god was the first and
most important commandment of the primitive religion.

Another objection to our hypothesis could be derived from
the hypothesis itself. If the tephillin, prepared from the hide
of the ox, point to identification with the ancient bull totem
of the Hebrew tribes, how can we explain the sacral character of the tallith (and, for that matter, the zizzith), which
consist of sheep's wool? It is not difficult to dispose of this objection, if we refer to the evolution of totemism—that is, to
historical motives. The exchange of totems, the replacement
of one kind of animal totem by another, may be observed in
the course of history of many ancient peoples. In such cases
the old totem often persists for a long while unaltered, or
acquires a different value when the new totem has victori-
ously established itself. Thus, for the initiated there is nothing surprising in the coexistence of tallith and tephillin.

Religious usage ultimately points in the direction which we have already been following; the injunction to kiss the tephillin reminds us that the ancient Semites used to cover their religious symbols and idols with kisses. Their sacred stones, trees, etc., were not regarded by the Semites as images of the gods, but originally as the gods themselves.

The Hebrews who kissed the zizzith performed, in a barely recognizable form, the same religious act as is performed by the Arab who kisses the Kaaba or the pious Catholic who kisses the Pope's foot. The objection that here a lifeless object is in question is of course irrelevant. In the Catholic church the faithful pay their last homage to a deceased Pope in the same manner. The feet of the holy man protrude through the grille of the Chapel of the Sacrament so that for three days the pious are still able to kiss them.[96] The recollection of this original sign of religious veneration has long survived, in an extraordinarily different form. This is a fitting moment to recall again that the miracles recorded in the Gospels are effected by contact with the fringes of Christ's garment. These miracles are of the same nature as the miraculous results produced by the clothing of holy individuals, and as the therapeutic effects of tabooed objects.

Perhaps this is also the moment to suggest that the tallith is to be regarded as the prototype of the consecrated article of clothing which assures the Catholic of the forgiveness of sins, I mean the scapular. We know that the wearing of the scapular is accompanied by numerous indulgences, just as the wearing of the tallith was felt to confer religious merit.[97]

We have now surveyed the hitherto unrecognized connection between the totemic disguises of primitive peoples and the ancient and the religious use of the tephillin and the tallith among the Israelites, as well as the analogous use of the scapular by the Catholics. In this connection a wealth of theologically interesting material presents itself, but here we must be content with the above-mentioned examples.

It may be noted, however, that in the light of our hypothesis Klein's old view of the subject, stressing the connection between the law of the Tephillin and other injunctions, is rehabilitated. It obviously cannot be a matter of indifference that the ritual should be mentioned in connection with the extremely ancient feast of Passover, and that it should be enjoined that the father should answer his son's question by informing him that the tephillin are tokens or memorials. The archaic nature of this feast is attested by many witnesses. The law that the passah must not be eaten raw points to an earlier custom of devouring the bloody and still-quivering flesh of the animal. Equally primitive are the spattering of the doorposts with blood, the old-fashioned nomadic garments, and the warning to leave some of the meat of the sacrifice until dawn of the following day.

There is no doubt that the animal slain and devoured was originally the sacrificed god, of whose flesh the clansmen ate in common, thereby renewing the community.[98] It now seems to us very reasonable that the law of the tephillin, which were evolved from the skin of the animal, should be connected with the festival of the great totemic banquet. The "it" which is to be shown to the sons as a sign or memorial is simply the divine hide, not the law, which belongs to a later period.

To be sure, in this injunction we are dealing with a metaphorical mode of speech, but behind it is concealed the old, original meaning, which was entirely objective—the identification with the old totemistic cattle-god.[99] This crude material interpretation which Stade and so many other scholars have confirmed leads us back in reality to the oldest religious stratum; i.e., to the horns of the totem of an ancient pagan religion.

Perhaps we shall also obtain an explanation of the enigmatic significance of totaphot, which, I believe, can really be derived from the root tâfa—to surround. Since to the scholars the meaning of "a band that goes around the head, a head-band" seemed improbable, and with reason, this etymological possibility was disregarded; as I think, too soon. Is no other explanation possible? The allusion to the encircling of the sacrificial beast about to be slain, an old Semitic practice, may suffice to make this explanation seem probable. Thus, the expression would indicate the connection of the tephillin with the national cultic feast of the Passover.[100]

We must not conclude this section without a few words to show how near the pious Jew who puts on the tallith and tephillin at his morning prayer is to the child who sticks a feather in his hair and plays at "Indians." What in the one case is done with the fervor of a religious exercise and in the other makes us smile at a childish game, had once all the gravity and seriousness of a vanished culture, which today seems to us alien and mysterious.

Returning to our point of departure, we can see why the Saviour reproved the pious with especial bitterness because "they make broad their phylacteries and enlarge the borders of their garments." They imagine themselves to be especially pious because they so conspicuously display the emblems of the living God. Here our reading of the matter coincides once more with the traditional interpretation of this passage of the Bible. Nevertheless, we do not believe that the way which we have followed was an unprofitable bypath.

VIII | Conclusion

We have, of course, every reason to think modestly of the upshot of these endeavors, for their essential result has been already foreshadowed by other psychoanalysts. As long ago as 1920 Karl Abraham had already explained the prayer shawl of the Jews as a substitute for the totemistically revered fleece of the ram.[101] Recently Frieda Fromm-Reichmann, basing her assertions on Abraham's investigations and on mine, has pointed out that the tephillin are the means of identification with the animal totem by wearing its hide and horns.[102] In this essay we have not been so concerned to claim priority for our thesis as to furnish, as far as possible, a scientific justification and proof of the assertions which are contained in those incidental and aphoristic observations.

Here we return to the special characterization and appreciation of the method applied in this inquiry, for the result which we have obtained we owe to the psychoanalytic mode of approach. Whatever the value of the result may prove, it could not have been obtained by the other methods at the disposal of the theologian. Our method consists in the psychological appreciation of otherwise unnoted and often barely perceptible details. Such a detail, hitherto absolutely unregarded, was the point of departure which led us to the comprehension of the significance of the tephillin. That detail was the tip of a hair that protruded from the head tephillah, which assuredly had not hitherto attracted the attention of any investigator. Here was a trace whose attentive psychoanalytic investigation led to a barely disputable archeological conclusion.

The analytic valuation of this hitherto unregarded detail seems in this case—and only in this special case—to justify the assertion which one so often hears repeated as a criticism of psychoanalytic investigations. Here the result obtained was really and truly dragged in by the hair! [103]

ELEVEN

THE SIGN LANGUAGE OF PRIESTLY BLESSING

1 | A furtive glance

The childhood memories published in this book are not the only ones that center around my grandfather. More than forty years ago I described how as a little boy I was taken by him several times to the synagogue on the Day of Atonement and heard there the ancient melody *Kol Nidre*, that made, though I did not know why, a lasting impression upon me.[1]

My teacher and friend Dr. Karl Abraham reviewed in an excellent essay, an article on the *Kol Nidre* I once wrote. I certainly did not deserve his praise, but he constructively criticized the fact that I had considered the prayer in isolation instead of viewing it as part of the complete ritual of the day.[2]

Abraham's benevolent and so-justified criticism helped me to call to mind another experience from that service: the priestly blessing. This ceremony takes place when the evening of the Day of Atonement approaches. The liturgy increases in solemnity toward that time. The priest pulls the prayer shawl over his head so that his face is concealed; he raises both hands, blessing the community with fingers spread.

I was told by my grandfather that I must not look at the priest while he speaks the blessing. He ordered me to cover my eyes with my hands during this time. I did as I was told, but I furtively glanced through the slits of my hands.

I am inclined to assume that my critical attitude toward religion took its departure in that act of the disobedience of the little boy. Every criticism starts as an observation, and to look where it is forbidden is irreverent. More than this— such a furtive, forbidden glance is an act of aggression, because its purpose is to discover the faults or weaknesses of the observed object. Our language sometimes reveals that aggressive character of looking. Do we not speak of staring at something and of looking daggers?

Disobeying my grandfather was certainly a rebellious deed, and I must have felt guilty about it. But of more importance was the fact that this was the irreverent curiosity I betrayed in looking. Yet it was perhaps an early manifestation of the inquisitiveness that is at the root of scientific pursuit and of the desire for research.

11 | The pantomime

The priestly blessing is an old ceremony, a residue of the Temple cult called *Birka kohanim*. Ismar Elbogen tells us that the priests at the time raised their hands to their heads in the temple, but outside only to the shoulders.[3] Akiba had already declared it improper to look at the priest when he speaks the blessing.[4]

There is a special significance connected with the priestly blessing because the priests are required to take off their sandals and wash their hands before it and to stand opposite the congregation when they speak the blessing and spread their fingers. Looking at the priest while he does this is believed to have a magical effect and is therefore forbidden. Yet the spreading of the hands is considered a characteristic symbol of the Aaronites or of the priests, and is often carved on their tombstones. Here is a contradiction which we are not—or are not yet—able to resolve.

We have noted that the Kohanim or the priests pull their prayer shawl over their heads and spread their hands when they recite the blessing. The third and the fourth fingers of the hand must be held together and be held separately from the other fingers. This unnatural position must be retained during the whole long ceremony.

To explain this gesture—or should I say pantomime?— Karl Abraham points to the passages in the eleventh chapter of Leviticus (11:3-8) in which is set forth which animals may be used as food and which are forbidden to be eaten: "Whatsoever parteth the hoof and is cloven-footed and cheweth the cud, among the beast, that shall ye eat. Nevertheless these shall ye not eat of them that chew the cud, or of them that divide the hoof: as the camel because he cheweth the cud, but divideth not the hoof; he is unclean unto you." [5] Among the four-footed animals created with cloven hoofs is the ram. The ram was once the sacred totem animal of the Hebrew tribes.[6]

We know that the primitive tribes of Australia and Africa identify with their totems, wrap themselves in their skins, imitate their movements and mimic them in every way.

In the priestly blessing the Kohanim or the priest imitated by the separation of the fingers the cloven hoofs of the ram of the sacred totem. The priest is in this situation equated with the totem animal, therefore with the primitive god of the Hebrew tribes. The hands of the priest are, as it were, the displaced feet of the totem animal. He himself is in this moment not a representative of God, but God himself— the god of an unremembered prehistoric time of the Hebrew tribes. When the priest whose face is concealed by the prayer-shawl, made of the skin of the ram, performs the gesture of the cloven hoofs with his hands, he has himself become the ram.

Karl Abraham arrived at this conclusion, but he does not mention that prohibition of looking at the priest reciting the blessing. How did that "strange notion," as Ismar El-bogen calls it, emerge and what is its significance? The priest stands opposite the congregation and makes that sign. He does not only represent, he *is* the totem god who shows himself to his worshipers. What then could be the meaning of forbidding them to look at him at this moment? Such a prohibition seems contradictory and paradoxical. I see only one way to resolve this perplexing paradox, if the premise of God's presence is upheld. The interdiction derives from a later time and is the result of a development that was already very remote from the area of primitive totemism. That means, from a phase that had replaced the rude notion of a totem animal or god by the idea of an invisible god. Let me use a comparison: let us assume that an artist, in this case a prominent mimic like Charlie Chaplin, gives a performance. While the audience is fascinated by the artist, the police appear and forbid the performance because, for instance, the gestures of the mimic amount to a caricature of the Kaiser.

Speaking now without metaphor, the pantomime of the priest in the role of the totem-god should not be seen because it was incompatible with the much later and superior conception of an invisible and incorporeal, disembodied God. What the priest showed in his blessing was the image of an ancient, discarded deity and not that of Yahweh, whose essential character was that of incorporeality. The God of Moses could be heard but not seen.[7]

It would not contradict this assumption that the gesture of the spread hands appears on many tombstones of the Aaronites. The priest reciting the blessing to the congregation represents or rather *is* the living god and speaks with God's voice. In his grave he is still deserving of reverence, but not of worship. That gesture engraved on his tombstone is not dangerous any longer. Only a living god is important.

But what was the danger when the priest stood in the synagogue and blessed, with hands spread out, the congregation whose god he was at this moment? What would be the reaction of the congregation confronted with the image of a barbarous god of the totem-animal?

The danger is to be compared in its character to the exclamation of the child in Andersen's fairy tale, revealing that the Emperor has no clothes on at all.

TWELVE

FAMILY SOLIDARITY

1 | Introduction

Whenever I am unsure of the validity or the value of my writings—and this is more frequent than I sometimes admit to myself—I ask my old friend Otto for his opinion. Otto is an internist with a flourishing practice, and many interests besides medicine. He is a keen and convincing critic. We are of the same age, and his Viennese Jewish background is the same as mine. He is not argumentative and even when we agree to disagree we understand each other. On certain occasions I have the feeling that he glances over my shoulders while I am working on a paper.

When my manuscript arrived at the preceding chapter, I asked him to read it. When he visited me, he first said a few appreciative words about it, but I knew, of course, that they were only preliminary and his essential criticism would follow them. He turned to the ritual of lighting his cigar.

"Well?" I asked.

"I hesitate because you might feel hurt and then you become easily aggressive."

"*Cet animal est très méchant; quand on l'attaque, il se défend*" I quoted. He ignored that and said cautiously: "I have two objections to the major part of these papers. The one concerns their style and the other the impression that they might evoke in the average reader."

"You mean the personalized or subjective character of the writing with which my psychoanalytic colleagues find fault?" I asked.

He thoughtfully observed the smoke rings of the cigar. "That's an old story. . . . No, I mean something more essential, that touches the core of your style—the building-up, the structure of those essays. They are represented as if they were mystery stories. Once you really introduce a kind of detective story."

"Only as a comparison," I defended myself.

"Admitted, but it might rub the reader the wrong way. He recognizes that you like that form of presenting a puzzling phenomenon and then you like to unscramble it with the help of historical and psychoanalytic explanations."

"Yes, that is true, but it is the nature of the material that makes it necessary for the investigation to go backwards. Think of presenting, for instance, a case of obsessional symptoms. There is first the representation of some puzzling trains of thoughts and compulsions. You have to go back before you

can go forward. But you know Freud's case histories——
What is the other objection?"

Otto took the cigar from his mouth and pointed it at me:
"It is rather a question I would like to ask you. Don't you
think that many readers of this book may feel that you are ut-
terly alienated from Judaism? The tone you adopt when you
discuss those pagan remnants is, it seems to me, so irritating
and negative that one might assume an anti-Semite has written some of the pages, especially those recollections of your
grandfather. Yes, I have even heard someone say that you
are anti-Semitic. Why do you always emphasize the obsolete
and negative side? Is there nothing valuable and even admirable in those residuals?"

I tried to explain, "I simply explore those heathen remnants and represent my psychoanalytic conclusions."

"But this should be possible without a critical note,
shouldn't it?" Otto objected. "Can't you ever see the good
side of things?"

I looked at him and said gently but firmly: "You can't eat
your cake—or rather your sholet—and have it too. I consider
the suggestion of anti-Semitism beneath contempt. You know
that I am an atheist, as Freud was, but I consider the Jews my
people and I feel as he did that the essence of my personality
is Jewish."

After Otto had left, I thought that some of the critical
things he had said about my writings were infuriatingly true.
He had certainly touched some tender spots. Then I realized
all of a sudden that I had made a decision some time back
without knowing it. An unexpected thought popped up while
I had listened to his criticism. I remembered that I had once,
many years ago, jotted down the outline of a paper about
Jewish family solidarity and about particularities of the
Mishpacha. I found that outline and surprisingly numerous
notes on the subject in one of the folders buried in a compartment of my desk.

That sudden flash of thought had the character of an un-spoken argument in our discussion. Here was the remnant of a prehistoric past of Israel that has continued until now and is still a most precious heritage from her primal times.

I decided to pick up that deserted research project. The next weeks were occupied with reading the pertinent litera-ture—or rather a part of it—and with writing the first draft. While I worked I sometimes remembered that discussion and thought to myself: what will Otto say now? He is cer-tainly on the side of the angels. It is a pity that there are no angels.

11 | Myth or fact?

A modern sociologist, Bess V. Cunningham, observed [1] that the patriarchal character of the Jewish family rooted in Bib-lical times "seems to be able to maintain greater solidarity than is shown by many other groups" and adds that this "may prove to be the greatest contribution of the Jews to modern life." [2] The same writer had already on a previous occasion remarked that "one very strong element in Jewish culture which differentiates it from Christian culture is the cohesiveness of the Hebrew family."

If this statement is correct, one may wonder why this pe-culiarity of Jewish family life has not become a subject of scientific research. There has been, of course, enough written about it. Historians and sociologists, Biblical scholars and archeologists have described the phenomena of Jewish fam-ily cohesiveness and group loyalty. The facts seemed un-deniable, but they were interpreted differently by Jews and anti-Semites. When Heinrich Heine celebrated this special Jewish quality, the Nazi "litérateurs" saw it as a hostile and malignant conspiracy against the other, non-Jewish people.

There is, however, no scarcity of literature on this subject. Contemporary Gentile scientists have also occasionally formulated their impressions on the subject.[3]

Yet it remained virginal scientific research; we do not know the origin of that family solidarity. We do not know its historical and psychological causes and we do not know if it will continue and if it is durable. The last question has frequently been posed by modern observers of Jewish life. They have pointed out that many factors seem to change radically the character of Jewish life. There are the different attitudes of young people toward their parents in the last decades, the weakening of the religious beliefs, the loosening of bonds between family members through the upheaval caused by the Nazis, the change in the position of the woman by the feminist movement, and so on. Mixed marriages have disrupted the traditional pattern of family life. Other social and economic factors bring about dramatic changes that make the stability of Jewish family life highly problematical in the next decades. Whatever the future may bring, the past cannot be disavowed: the closeness of the Jewish family was a fact.

Since the Lord said to the first couple: "Be fruitful and multiply" (Gen. 1:28), the Hebrew family (about which more will be said later on) has desired children. When Yahweh promised the first Hebrew great rewards, Abraham said, "Lord God, what whilt thou give me, seeing I am childless?" (Gen. 15:2). In the Talmudic age and later, Jewish family life was based on mutual respect between parents and children.

The other day I heard a rabbi say "It is easy enough to love your father and mother, but not so easy to honor them." The Talmud says "Great is the honoring of father and mother, for God makes more of it than of honoring Himself." [4] The commandment (Exod. 20:12) "Honor thy father and thy mother that thy days may be long upon the land which the

Lord thy God giveth thee" promises a long life not to the individual but to the people. It concerns the life—or rather the survival—of many generations.

With these remarks we have already entered the area of the connection between the individual and the group to which he belongs. I. Abrahams points out that Jewish family life has retained a distinct character and forms an intimate bond between the individual and the community. "Family solidarity, in its aspects of piety and altruism, led to the establishment at once of a primate code of morality and a communal linking of the generations." The individual was merged in the family, the family was merged in the community. "Every Jew found his joy and sorrow in all Jews' joys and sorrows." [5]

The psychological significance of intimate family life is described by Heinrich Heine. He considered the Jewish home "a haven of rest from the storms that raged round the very gates of the ghetto, nay, a fairy palace in which the spattered objects of the mob's derision threw off their garb of shame and resumed the royal attire of freemen. The home was the place where the Jew was at his best. In the market place he was perhaps hard and sometimes ignoble; in the world he helped his judges to misunderstand him; in the home he was himself." [6]

Since Heine wrote these lines, more than a hundred years have passed. How much of this Jewish family solidarity has survived the social and economical changes since? Is that solidarity still a fact or is it a myth?

III | The lower and the middle classes

The heading of the preceding section, Myth or Fact?, is the subtitle of an excellent sociological inquiry into Jewish family solidarity. The author of that book, Stanley R. Brav, introduces his inquiry with the remark that some current fiction gives the impression that the traditional beauty of Jewish family life has become vitiated.[7] Yet, he continues, "These stories appear to be merely the occasional aberration from a typical situation."

Brav's comparative study draws a parallel between Jewish and Gentile family life in Vicksburg, a small community on the Mississippi. Applying statistical and other methods, he arrives at valuable conclusions followed by clear insights into the differences of the two groups. He compares, for instance, the different degree of attachment between individual family members and group loyalty, conceived as a second major constituent of family cohesiveness. It is, moreover, remarkable how often the sayings of dear departed ones are quoted ("My Mother Selig used to say"). Their influence is still vividly felt many years after their death. The parental pride in children's achievement is also noticeable here. Here an old tradition is continued. Proverbs (17:6) says: "Children's children are the crown of old men/ And the glory of children are their fathers."

The research worker finds that group loyalty, as registered in the influence of deceased relatives' words and in pride in the accomplishments of family members—particularly children—is stronger in the average "Jewish group than in the selected non-Jewish samples." [8] Brav compares Jewish married couples and their family patterns with "normal" non-Jewish couples in that small community and gives credence to the popular assumptions of strength in Jewish family solidarity.

With regard to group loyalty he states that members in the community have signed affidavits of support for relatives, many of whom they have never seen, who happened to live in Austria and Czechoslovakia.[9] Others have sent allowances for the support of poor relatives in the old country for long periods and have spent large sums of money to bring others to America and to help them to adjust.

The other day I saw a cartoon showing a little girl who is dragging a little boy to Hebrew school. "I don't like it either, David," she says, "but we have to for our children's sake." All for the children! Jewish readiness for sacrifices and self-deprivations is especially remarkable in the case of parents who give all to seek the happiness and success of their children. (Sigmund Freud wrote to S. Ferenzi [July 7, 1913] of "the assurance that the children will be provided for which for a Jewish father is a matter of life and death.")[10]

The inquirer does not forget to mention the occasional drawbacks of this attitude and observes, for instance, that the exaggerated parental solicitude produces "spoiled Jewish children." Jewish family solidarity and group loyalty—the result of this sociological study—is greater by comparison than those in the non-Jewish community. These findings concern the middle and lower Jewish classes in the South. But are the same qualities to be found in the very rich Jews, and in the very wealthy ones who live in the capitals of the world?

I V | The Rothschild *mischpacha*

Frederic Morton remarks in his excellent family portrait, *The Rothschilds,* that it is almost impossible "to meet a present-day Rothschild without first meeting his forefathers." [11] The house and anterooms of his office are filled with paintings, busts, reliefs of his ancestors, among them invariably that of the little Mayer of the Frankfurt am Main ghetto, so to speak the ancestor of the family. Mayer would have been a bit of that Jewish flotsam and nothing more, if he had had no sons as a "power investment." But he had sons and his work became the "perfect seed for his children to grow and pluck—and all their tireless harvesting toil would be but new sowing for their children and their children's children."

In the house of Rothschild, brilliance was often individual, but accomplishment was joint. The brothers lived in different countries, in Paris, in London, in Frankfurt am Main, but they never lost contact with each other and they worked together. There is a story reporting that one of the brothers, Nathan, was asked by his small son how many different nations there were in the world. "There are only two you need bother about," Nathan said. "There is the mischpacha and there are the others." Morton justly puts "The Family" into capital letters because the Rothschilds spoke of it this way.[12]

To the end of her life, Gutele Rothschild, the dowager empress who died at the age of ninety-six, had to see the persons who married into the mischpacha. All nuptials had to be celebrated at Frankfurt am Main or the new member had at least to see Gutele in the cornerhouse of that old ghetto to be appraised and approved by the old lady.

When Nathan died in 1836, shortly after his oldest son's wedding in Frankfurt, he called his children to his bedside and told them that it was not important whether one of his sons had a few hundred thousand pounds more than the other. "All that mattered was that they should hold together in unity."

Besides family solidarity two features are common to the brothers: their loyalty to their people and their charitableness. Lord Nathanael Mayer Rothschild did not change his name, as so many Jews did the whole world over. "No persecution or pogram occurred anywhere without thunder from New Court against the oppressors, without aid to the victims."[13] Russia, cruel to her Jews, asked in vain for money from the Rothschilds.

The charitable donations of the Family became gigantic.

Nathanael had a special, amply staffed department at New Court to handle all donations to Jewish and Gentile philanthropic organizations.

There was the fundamental Rothschild desire, called absurd by Bismarck, "to leave to each of their [often numerous] children as much as they themselves inherited." Besides that, however, was the wish that the family solidarity should be maintained.

When Anselm Rothschild died, he left a will that sounds like "an exact echo of the first patriarch's will composed under a ghetto roof nearly three quarters of a century before." [14] Anselm wrote "I charge all my dear children to live constantly in harmony, not to allow family ties to loosen, to avoid all dispute and unpleasantness and legal actions, to exercise forbearance and tolerance to one another and not let themselves be carried away by angry passion." He asked his children to follow "the example of their splendid grandparents for those qualities have always insured the happiness and prosperity of the whole Rothschild family, and may my dear children never become unmindful of this family spirit." They never have, to this day.

Does it not seem as if that family solidarity and loyalty to the clan pervades poor middle-class and rich Jews? Is it an enduring heritage?

v | Little interlude

I wondered why Frederic Morton did not mention an excellent joke of Heinrich Heine. In his "Bäder von Lucca," the poor Hirsch Hyazinth who keeps a lottery office boasts that he sat beside the great Solomon Rothschild, who "treated me entirely as his equal, quite famillionairly"—entirely familiarly, that is, as far as a millionaire can treat a poor relative. The tone of bitterness is unmistakable. Yet Hirsch Hyazinth is proud of his intimacy with Rothschild.

To tell the truth, the only quality one misses in the many descriptions and characterizations of typical Jewish family life is that of intimacy. This means that there is not only that special closeness and mutual psychological understanding between members of the family, but also between them and those who are expected to join the family circle.

Abrahams points out that the confined quarters occupied by the Jews in the Middle Ages, as well as the survival of patriarchal sentiments, often led to the dwelling of the whole family, of several generations, under the same roof.[15] This local nearness certainly favored that intimacy of relations, but also economic factors sometimes promoted it. After marriage, the parents-in-law frequently provided accomodation for their son-in-law or at least financially supported the young couple during the first years of marriage.

This was also the case with the young couple of whom I shall now write. This example also gives me an opportunity to show how an outsider is accepted and later taken into the family circle and its warm atmosphere of intimacy.

The following report follows the account of a woman who became a patient of mine and told me in her psychoanalytic sessions about her girlhood years: "Mama used to say: 'The man whom you want to marry has still to be born.' She meant I was too critical of all young men who took me out. I asked her: 'How do you know that you're in love, Ma?' 'Only wait, you will know yourself,' she said.

"I was then secretary in a company and I heard that a young man from Detroit would get a leading position in our New York office. When he arrived, I immediately fell in love with him. All the girls in our office were setting their caps for him. He took many of them out. They said he took girls out as soon as he learned to walk. He also invited me for dinner several times, but I had decided to give him a run for his money and told him I had other dates. He stopped asking me then. What could I do? I couldn't invite him, could I?

"Once we stepped into the elevator at the same time and I casually said 'You invited me to dinner; when will you take me?' 'Tomorrow, if you are free.' I was free, of course, and I had already decided to get him, if it was the last thing I did. He took me to dinner then each Friday, but Mama always asked me to bring him home. Finally she decided I should not go out with him again before he had been in our house for dinner at least once. When he asked me the next time I said I could not go. I then said I had to ask Mama first. That was in his office and he pointed to the telephone and said 'Speak with her!' I called her, but she was adamant.

"He did not hear what she said, of course, but he must have guessed it because he said, 'Oh, I am going to be inspected.' Then I rang up Mama again and told her that he would come on Friday evening. He asked me before that whether we would have to stay there a long time after dinner or if we could go to a movie afterward. You see, he was afraid that he would be bored with my family. We even agreed upon a signal: if he wanted to leave and go to a movie or dancing with me, he would yawn. He never did. He liked Mama very much. I played the piano for him and my father and my brother talked business with him. He stayed until after midnight.

"When he left, Mama said: 'You live alone, don't you? I will give you something to eat that you can take home.' She went to the kitchen and filled some jars with knishes and meat loaf. He came many times to the house. Once when he was there, my father whispered to me: 'If you don't get him, Mama will.'

"Then he had to go to a convention in Milwaukee for two weeks. I asked him 'Will you write me?' He promised to write, but I never got a letter or even a post card from him.

"When he returned, he called me into his office. 'Why?' I

said, 'I thought you were not interested in me any longer.' 'Why should you think that?' he asked, 'You did not write me even once.' I said. 'I did', he said and took from his pocket some post cards with my address on them. He had not sent them. 'How could I?' he said, 'You don't write this on post cards. Will you marry me, Jane?'

"When I came home that evening, I went straight to the bedroom of Mama and Papa and said: 'I shall marry.' And they both had only one thing to ask: 'When?' "

We see here that the new member is as completely absorbed by the family as a foreign body by an amoeba.

What interests me are rather the potentialities of this family solidarity than its achievements. Is it not imaginable that the best features of it will one day be transferred from its narrow circle to the family of man?

V I | Hypothesis

A clinical psychologist recently published a paper which he subtitled "Five hypotheses in search of a theory." [16] There are less than five hypotheses about the roots and reasons for Jewish family solidarity and there is scarcely any serious and valid psychological theory explaining the phenomenon. There are, of course, some explanations, but they are persuasive rather than convincing and their formulation is not particularly useful.

Again and again it is pointed out that the community of aims and interests ties the members of the Jewish family together. Then there is the repeated reference to the conditions in which Jews lived, to their confined quarters and to the bitter hostility of their environment. One hundred twenty-five years ago Heinrich Heine had already advanced the argument in his little treatise *Shakespeare's Girls and*

Women in this form: "Pushed out from public life and from Christian society, only family feelings remained to the poor Jew and they appear in him with the most touching tenderness." [17] He is speaking of Shylock and Jessica.

The other reference points to the laws of the Bible as to one of the roots of family solidarity. This reference as well as the one to the crowding in the ghetto were given as explanation of the cohesiveness of Jewish family life. There is no doubt that those factors contributed to family solidarity, but it is certain that they are not sufficient to explain its origin and character. The sociologists and historians who are satisfied with this explanation accomplished not much more than pigeonholing the situation. The French have a neat phrase for such casual and mock-scientific dismissal of fact. They call it *une affaire classée*.

I have no quarrel with those scholars who refer to the crowded quarters of the ghetto, to the persecution of the Jews, and to the observance of the Biblical law, but these factors are merely contributing ones and do not possess the significance attributed to them. Let me use a comparison to make the meaning of this clear: a psychoanalyst observes that his patient John behaves in a certain manner when in definite social conditions. It is tempting to assume that the reaction of John, who is now a man of, let us say, thirty years, is conditioned by that social position or situation. But the progressing psychoanalytic process reveals that John has already showed exactly the same behavior when he was a boy of eight. We shall then assume that this kind of reaction and behavior was determined in previous experiences without, of course, perhaps excluding the impact of later conditions that had a qualifying influence upon his behavior.

In other words, I think that those historians and sociologists date the origin of family solidarity and group loyalty too late in the Middle Ages or in the later period of the Diaspora. The wellspring of that special family solidarity is to be searched for in a phase at least two thousand years earlier. There are more reasons for it than are dreamed of in our sociological philosophy.

What is presented in the following pages is not a psychoanalytic theory—not even a hypothesis—on the origin of Hebrew family solidarity, but a historic sketch of its earliest development. As such it is a necessary study for a psychoanalytic investigation. A psychoanalyst who studies the behavior of his patient has to go back into earlier years, into adolescence and childhood in order to understand him. It is the same with the peculiarities of groups and nations. Without inquiry into earlier phases, an understanding of the present condition is excluded. An exploration undertaken to answer the question *Why?* has first to ascertain the *How?* the manner in which a certain situation unfolded.[18]

VII | The prehistoric roots

My confident advocacy of historic—or rather prehistoric— circumstances as a primary agent of family solidarity will be understood by a presentation of the social conditions of early Israel. It is true that we know little about it, we guess more and hope that new findings will advance our knowledge.

It seems almost certain that the tribe (Hebrew: *matteh*) was not the oldest group of Israel's organization, but the clan (*-mischpachah*, from Hebrew *schafah*—to extend). Louis-Germain Levy, who explored the social groups of ancient Israel, arrives at the conjecture that in the earlier times the tribe developed from the clan (*-mischpachah*) or resulted from the union of various clans.[19] Thus the tribe is not the oldest Hebrew group, but the patriarchal Hebrew mischpachah that encompassed, in extreme cases, a few hundred people. (The family of Jacob numbered seventy heads—Exodus 1:5).

It is likely that in early phases the tribe that was only an expanded clan, had the character of a family. There is a difference between the clan and the family in a narrow sense, although the same word often signifies the one and the other. The family in a restricted sense is called *bayith* (household). The mischpachah is much larger and more complex than the household (parents, children, servants). In Numeri there is a strict difference made between the tribe, the mischpachah, and the paternal house, although the tribe is a group of numerous mischpachoth and the mischpachah is the ensemble of several paternal houses.

The differences between this ancient grouping and ours is so great that the reference to the scholarly work of J. Petersen[20] will be advantageous in the interest of clarification. Petersen considers the mischpachah (clan or family) a connecting link between the tribe and the household or father's house. The mischpachah is to be regarded as an expanded household and is more limited than the tribe. Yet the line of distinction between tribe and family is sometimes fluid. The Danites, who generally form a tribe, are sometimes called a family (Judges 13:2, 18:11).

Tribe was thus a living term, but was not essentially different from the family. The last term is applied to those who are of common blood or, as the Hebrews say "of common flesh." They considered those of common flesh as of common character, equipped with the same essential features. Israel is a confederation of families. The two kingdoms are two families (Jer. 33:24). "Nay," says Petersen, "the whole people is one mischpachah, one family as against all the other families of the earth," [21] and he points to the words of the Lord (Amos 3:2), "You only have I known of all the families of the earth."

Whenever Israel wants to define a community, she uses

the expression *Mischpachah,* and no other social definitions is so living as this. The tribe becomes a territory and the house is conceived as the household, but the family is determined by kinship; they have the "common stamp."

How flexible the term is can be seen by the following instances: Micah thunders against the Israelites as one family (2:3). Jeremiah speaks of them as "this evil family" (8:3). Amos (3:1) speaks to the family "who were brought up from the land of Egypt." The term designates not only those of common flesh and blood, but also a "psychic community" throughout the ages.[22]

The patriarchal history as it is represented in the Old Testament is a family history. The unity of the house remains as long as there are any descendants of the father. In II. Sam. (9:3), David asks "Is there yet any that is left of the house of Saul that I may show him kindness for Jonathan's sake?" He is told that Mephibosheth, Jonathan's son, is still alive. Mephibosheth is a grown man, but he is still considered of the house of Saul.

When a man is going to die he sets his house in order (Isaiah 38) and his will is conveyed to posterity. The continuity of the generations is thus maintained.

Kinship in the first line is determined by consanguinity. David says that the Judaeans are his brothers, his bone and flesh (II Sam. 19:13). Yet all Israel is conceived as a family. Therefore all Israelites are considered brothers. (Ex. 2:11; Lev. 10:6; II Sam. 19:41-44; Jer. 34:14).

Speaking of an old man, Petersen describes him as satisfied, if he sees that his blessing is acting undiminished in the family: "then he lies down calmly, for in the family his life is lived and his blessing acts. Against the life of the family that of the individual does not mean more than the burned out twigs falling from the fire."[23] The local nearness of the graves to the house indicates the unbroken connection between the living and the dead. The survivors remain, so to speak, in touch with the departed. "There is a firm unity between the departed and the surviving kinsmen which is maintained."

The memory of the departed lives on. When he is more and more forgotten, "he is merged entirely in the great stock of life which uphold the family, that which is called the fathers. From them he has sprung and to them he returns." [24]

Although W. R. Smith's *The Religion of the Semites* appeared in 1889, the views of the excellent scholar are still valuable. He points out that kinship is an older thing than family life and in the most primitive societies was not a subdivision of the clan, but contained members of more than one kindred. The family meal never became a fixed institution among Semites generally. The fathers rarely ate with their wives and children. Smith assumes that the origin of these customs was formed at a time when a man and his wife were not usually of one kin and when only kinsmen would eat together.[25]

The idea of kinship is central to Smith's view of ancient Semitic life. In a case of murder, Arabian tribesman do not say "The blood of M. of N. has been spilled," naming the man; they say "Our blood has been spilled." The Hebrew phrase claiming kinship is "I am your bone and your flesh" (Lev. 25:49). In Hebrew as in Arabic the sentence designates one's clan or kindred group.

What constitutes kinship? In the first place, of course, consanguinity, but also sharing a meal with another person. Those who eat together are of the same blood, of the same substance. The clanmen are blood brothers and are united. It may dawn on us that the kinship system was the model after which significant human contacts were formed later on. Even a late phrase as the French sentence *Les amis de mes amis sont mes amis* is patterned after this prototype.

VIII | The roots of group loyalty

If this historic or prehistoric view of ancient Semitic life is
accurate, we doubt that the economic and social conditions
of medieval Jewry were responsible for the peculiarity of
family solidarity and group loyalty. As mentioned before, we
do not deny their impact, especially with regard to maintain-
ing those attitudes. Yet those factors are only contributory
ones and continue and intensify earlier tendencies whose
roots reach deeper into the dark subsoil of the past. The social organization of the ancient Semitic tribes provides the
key to the understanding of that special solidarity and loyalty.

In this context Smith's reference to the common meal is
important, because it points to the intimate connection between food and religion. Religion was once not a private af-
fair as it is for us today, but a community unity based on belonging to the same totem clan. The totem membership was
decisive for what one was allowed to eat and what was forbidden for one to relish later on, for food preferences and avoidances.

That intimate connection between religion and food still
resounds in Shylock's words "I will buy with you, sell with
you, talk with you, walk with you, and so following, but I will
not eat with you, drink with you, nor pray with you" (*The
Merchant of Venice*).

Don Isaac Abarbanel in Heinrich Heine's *Rabbi of Ba-
charach* is a renegade, but he regularly goes to the ghetto. "It
is not to pray," he declares "but to eat that I visit Jew Street."
In that food predeliction the renegade still remains faithful
to Judaism, that means to an older and more primitive form
of Hebrew religion.

The two activities of worship and common eating were once almost identical. The messmates were united by oral identifications. Not the family that prays together, but the one that eats together.

I have tried to trace the peculiarities of Jewish family solidarity and group loyalty back to the ancient Semitic notion of kinship. Kinship is produced by consanguinity and by common meals.

The reference to those two factors, determined by specific life experiences of Hebrew tribes, is certainly only a preparation for research into the causes of family solidarity and group loyalty which is not only an emotional experience of intimate contact, but also of engagement and commitment.

At this point I would like to discontinue this research into the historic or prehistoric conditions of those typical Jewish attitudes. The views presented here are only a minority opinion. They do not pretend to be a theory, but form an initial preparation for some. They are only an attempt to provide bricks from which a theory may eventually be constructed. For this writer it is enough to climb a few steps nearer to the truth that will be reached by younger men, not yet bothered by shortness of breath in mountain climbing.

EPILOGUE

When the manuscript of this book was finished, something strange happened to me: I recovered a letter from Freud which I had misplaced and missed for some years. The letter, which was in reply to a question, was written a few weeks before Freud's death. Here is the German text.*

> 13.6.1939
> 20 Maresfield Gardens
> London N.W.3

Geehrter Herr Doktor

    Wenn Sie sich von dem Abdruck meiner damaligen Äusserung über Lear einen Vorteil für Ihre neue Arbeit erwarten, bin ich

* By permission of Sigmund Freud Copyrights, Ltd., London.

nicht in Ihrem Weg. An und für sich scheint sie mir weder sehr tiefgründig noch unzweifelhaft richtig zu sein. Ich wäre also auch nicht zu entänscht wenn Sie sie nicht erwähnen oder aber auf den einen Satz beschränken würden, dass man Lear nicht gut einen Hysteriker nennen kann. Ich vermute da tiefere persönliche Zusammenhänge die ich noch nie dargestellt habe, auch jetzt nicht behandeln möchte.

Ihr sehr ergebener

Freud

Dear Doctor:

If you expect some advantage for your new paper from the publication of my past statement about Lear, I will not stand in your way. Considered by itself it seems to me neither very profound nor correct beyond any doubt. Thus I would also not be too disappointed if you would not mention, or would limit it to the single sentence that one cannot well call Lear hysterical. I suspect there are deeper personal reasons which I have never presented. I would also prefer not to touch on them now.

Yours very sincerely,

Freud

After I had found this letter again, I tried to remember the statement about Lear that Freud had made many years ago and the details of our conversation. Only a few features were recalled. I remembered that I had then wanted to write a paper about the insane figures in Shakespeare's plays. The idea was that in many scenes those psychotic figures say things that seem to reveal that they are looking at themselves, as if they were, so to speak, *observateurs de soi-même*. At first I thought, of course, of Hamlet's sham insanity. I remember that I discovered such features also in *Lear*, for instance in the King's lines in the fourth act:

I am a very foolish fond old man,
Fourscore and upward, not an hour more nor less;

And, to deal plainly,
I fear I am not in my perfect mind.

and in those touching words:

For, as I am a man, I think this lady
To be my child Cordelia.

That projected paper was never written, by the way, and is
not important. Only what Freud said in that conversation is
of consequence. It must have been in 1930 or 1931. I remember I came to Vienna on one of my frequent visits from Hol-
land where I then lived. We spoke of the question of the real
or pretended insanity of some of Shakespeare's characters.
Lear was mentioned and Freud told me that the King was
not hysterical.[1]

I have a visual image of Freud sitting across from me in his
consultation room. My glance now strays to the framed lines
of Rudyard Kipling in the corner of my own room:

If you can think
and not make thought your aim. . . .

I give myself over to thought-associations. In 1930 or 1931
. . . I was then forty-two years old and Freud was seventy-
four years old. The old Goethe. . . . How does Goethe
come into this context? He looked up to Shakespeare "as to a
higher human being." . . . His conversations with Ecker-
mann. . . . But I do not remember that he said anything
about Lear. . . . The last lines of Freud's letter come back
to me. He speaks there of deeper personal connections or
relations which he would prefer not to discuss even now.

The letter Freud wrote to a British scholar about Lear
occurs to me. A thought hovers on the edge of consciousness,
but draws away from it, as though from something painful.
. . . I must look up that letter. There it is . . . to James

S. H. Bransom, March 25, 1934.[2] Freud had studied Bransom's book and agrees with the last section of it, which reveals the secret of the Lear tragedy: the King's incestuous claims on the daughter's love. Enough of those ancient wishes remain in the unconscious that a poet may dimly perceive them. Freud then discusses Lear's insanity as a rejection of those incestuous wishes in the sense: "only an insane person would have such desires." Freud considers it curious that in the play which deals with the father's relations to his three daughters, their mother is nowhere mentioned. ("After all there must have been one.")

I read that letter, of course, twenty years after Freud's death, but is it possible that Freud said something of a similar kind to me then? It is unlikely. I have two grown-up daughters myself. These are perhaps similar "personal" connections or reasons in me. . . . The emotional disengagement of old age—is that not the technical term psychiatrists use?—does not prevent one from experiencing grief, mortification or loneliness.

Loneliness! I have suddenly the visual image of Freud getting up from his chair and reaching for a book he wants to show me. . . . Goethe. Oh, here it is . . . it must have been a volume of Goethe's poems and in it some lines on Lear. . . . I know now. It was in the *Zahme Xenien*.

I get up from the chair (and I am aware of making the same slow motions that Freud had then) and search for that volume of Goethe among my books. I find the lines.

> Ein alter Mann ist stets ein König Lear!—
> Was Hand in Hand mitwirkte, stritt,
> Ist längst vorbeigegangen,
> Was mit und an dir liebte, litt,
> Has sich wo anders angehangen;
> Die Jugend ist um ihretwillen hier,
> Es wäre töricht zu verlangen:
> Komm, ältele du mit mir.

[An old man is always a King Lear!—
What worked and fought hand in hand
Is long past,
What loved with you, loved you, and suffered with you
Has attached itself elsewhere;
Youth is here for its own sake:
You can't demand—how foolish it would be—
"Come, become old with me!"]

I had read then those lines pointed out to me by Freud and had understood, of course, that they were the feelings of an old man, a man approaching death. I was about forty then. Of course, I had understood what he meant, but I only understood it with my head.

I now understand by experience. You live and learn . . .

I am now seventy-five and it seems so odd to feel as old as Freud was when he showed me Goethe's lines. Yes, these are the feelings of an old man, a man approaching death.

NOTES

ONE

A HOME AWAY FROM HOME

1. Theodor H. Gaster, *Festivals of the Jewish Year* (New York, 1952), p. 82,2 (sp.ct. P. 83).

2. Compare especially Mowinckel, "Drama" in *Religion in Geschichte und Gegenwart* (2d ed.; Tübingen, 1927), vol. I.

3. Gaster, *op. cit.*, p. 8.

4. Haayim Schauss, *The Jewish Festivals* (Cincinnati, 1938), p. 200.

5. J. Wensinck, *Arabic of Tabernacles* (Amsterdam, 1925), p. 29.

6. Schauss, *op. cit.*, p. 203.

7. Gaster, *op. cit.*, p. 84.

8. Schauss, *op. cit.*, p. 200.

9. Sukkah 11b.

10. *Thespis* (New York, 1950), p. 38.

11. Quoted from *The New York Times,* October 12, 1962.

12. *Arabic New Year and the Feast of Tabernacles* (Amsterdam, 1925).

13. P. 26.

14. *Gottesdienst in Israel* (München, 1954) (Studien zur Geschichte des Laubhüttenfestes).

15. *Prolegomena zur Geschichte Israels* (6th ed.; 1927).

16. A. Alt, *Zelte und Hütten* (Festschrift für F. Nötzschner, 1950).

17. *Gottesdienst in Israel* (München, 1954), p. 26.

18. From the speech made by Danton to the Legislative Committee of General Defense, September 2, 1792.

19. Frazer, *Folklore in the Old Testament* (abr. ed.; New York, 1927), p. ix.

20. John Gray, *Archaeology and the Old Testament* (London, 1962), p. 5.

21. *Myths, Dreams and Mysteries* (New York, 1960).

22. R. Thurnwald, *Primitive Initiation und Wiedergeburtsriten* (Eranos Jahrbuch, 1939), p. 393.

23. *Myths, Dreams and Mysteries* (New York, 1960), pp. 197ff.

24. Gaster, *op. cit.*, p. 96.

25. *Ibid.*

26. *Ibid.*

27. Schauss, *op. cit.*, p. 196.

28. Frazer, *The Belief in Immortality* (London, 1913), vol. I, p. 250.

TWO

"THIS IS MY KADDISH"

1. W. O. E. Oesterley and G. H. Box, *The Religion and Worship of the Synagogue* (London, 1907), p. 340.

2. Simon Cohn, "Ancestor Worship," *Universal Jewish Encyclopedia,* I, 298.

3. I Kings 11:36; II Kings 8:19; II Chron 21:27; Ps. 152:11.

4. "Kaddish," *Universal Jewish Encyclopedia,* VI, 214.

5. *Universal Jewish Encyclopedia,* VI, 274.

6. In his article on Jewish ancestor worship, *Encyclopedia of Religion and Ethics,* I, 459ff.

7. Reinach's article was first published in the *Revue des Études Juives,* XLI (1900) and can now be found in *Cults, Myths and Religions* (London, 1912).

8. In his article on Jewish ancestor worship, *Encyclopedia of Religion and Ethics,* I, 460.

9. *Ibid.*

10. Quoted from Otto Fennichel, *The Psychoanalytic Theory of Neurosis* (New York, 1945), p. 371.

11. *Moses and Monotheism* (New York, 1949), Part III, sec. iii.

12. *The Religion of Israel* (Chicago, 1960), p. 312.

13. Especially of certain acts of mourning. Compare Jer. 16:6, where mourners are reported to have mutilated themselves and the forbidding of such practice in Lev. 19:28; Deut. 14:1.

14. *Myth and Guilt, Mystery on the Mountain, The Creation of Woman, The Temptation.*

15. Robert Aron assumes that Jesus said Kaddish for his father Joseph (*Jesus of Nazareth: The Hidden Years* [New York, 1962], p. 214). In Jesus' time the Kaddish did not have the character of an intercessory

prayer but "he must have heard said and even pronounced it when he occupied Joseph's place in the synagogue and stood up to lament his absence."

In a scene from a new play *Suppose A Wedding* by Bernard Malamud (Farrar, Straus, New York), an old Jewish actor named Feuer speaks of the best roles he once acted—for instance, the part of Hamlet "der Yeshiva Bucher"—and adds "I was wonderful in the kaddish scene for his father."

In a recent study Rabbi Marvin Luban conceives of the Kaddish as "Man's reply to the problem of evil" since it is "instrumental in helping man overcome his grief in a positive manner" (*The Kaddish* [New York, 1962], p. 34).

THREE

STONES ON THE GRAVES OF JEWISH CEMETERIES

1. (New York, 1948), p. 91.

2. The correct phrases are "buried with his fathers" (I Kings 12:21) and "slept with his fathers" (I Kings 2:10).

3. Joseph Marcus in *Universal Jewish Encyclopedia*, V, 89.

4. Hobley, *Journal of the Anthropological Institute*, XXXII, 344.

5. Other instances of a similar kind are quoted by E. Sidney Hartland, *Encyclopedia of Religion and Ethics*, IV.

6. Gen. 23:19; 25:9; 49:31; 50:13.

7. Gen. 50:2, 26.

8. *Encyclopedia of Religion and Ethics*, IV, 497.

9. First published in 1889, London; new ed. 1894.

10. *Ibid.*, 204.

11. In his paper "Obsessive Act and Religious Practice," *Collected Papers*, II.

12. Ludwig Jekels, "The Problem of the Duplicated Expression of Psychic Themes," *Selected Papers* (New York, 1952), pp. 131ff.

13. *Of Love and Lust, Sex in Man and Woman, The Need to Be Loved,* all published by Farrar, Straus and Company, New York.

FOUR

A STRANGE CURSE

1. Gen. 37:29; I Sam. 4:12; I Kings 5:8.

2. *Folklore in the Old Testament* (London, 1919), pp. 227ff, 270ff.

3. *The Search Within* (New York, 1956), pp. 540ff.

4. *The Interpretation of Dreams* (New York, 1913); *Introductory Lectures to Psychoanalysis* (New York, 1920).

FIVE

ASHES

1. *The Principles of Sociology* (London, 1893).

2. H. H. Bancroft, *The Native Races of the Pacific States* (San Francisco, 1875-76), I, 397.

3. *Folklore in the Old Testament* (London, 1919), p. 298.

4. "Dust, Earth and Ashes as Symbols of Mourning among the Ancient Hebrews," *Journal of the American Oriental Society,* XX (1899).

5. "Mourning and Melancholia," *Collected Papers,* IV.

6. Hans Zullinger, "Beiträge zur Psychologie der Trauer und Bestattungsgebräuche," *Imago,* X (1924) and *Die Roitshaeggeten, Imago,* XIV (1928).

7. Gen. 3:19.

SIX

A FOOTNOTE ON MIRROR MAGIC

1. *The Golden Bough,* XVII, 11, and *Taboo and the Perils of the Soul,* pp. 94ff.

2. A. E. Crawley, "Mirror," *Encyclopedia of Religion and Ethics,* VIII, 696.

3. J. G. Lawson, *Modern Greek Folklore and Ancient Greek Religion* (Cambridge, 1910), p. 10.

4. *Spiegelzauber* (Leipzig and Vienna, 1919), pp. 207ff.

SEVEN

THE RE-EMERGING MOTHER-GODDESS

1. Otto Weber, *Arabien vor dem Islam* (Leipzig, 1901), p. 19.

2. Robert Briffault, *The Mothers* (New York, 1928), p. 32.

3. Otto Rank, *Das Inzestmotiv in Dichtung und Sage* (Leipzig, 1921), p. 317, and *Psychoanalytische Beiträge zur Mythenforschung* (2d ed.; Leipzig and Vienna, 1922), p. 77. I modified and completed Rank's theory in my *The Creation of Woman* (New York, 1960).

4. Eduard Meyer, *Der Papyrusfund von Elephantine* (2d ed.; Leipzig, 1912), p. 63, and A. Cook, *The Cambridge Ancient History,* I, 206.

5. Morris Jastrow, *Religion of Babylonia and Assyria* (New York, 1898), p. 104.

6. *Encyclopedia of Religion and Ethics,* V, 857.

7. *Religion of the Semites* (2d ed.; London, 1894), p. 52.

8. *Universal Jewish Encyclopedia,* X, 537.

9. *Ibid.*

10. More Nebuchum 1, 28.

11. In this description I am using Abraham J. Herschel's chapter on the mystical elements in Judaism, in Finkelstein (ed.), *The Jews* (Philadelphia, 1949).

12. *Ibid.*, pp. 613ff.

13. *Universal Jewish Encyclopedia*, IX, 296.

14. Herschel, *loc. cit.*, pp. 614ff.

15. Addendum 1963. When God destroyed the Temple, Abraham rose up as a complainant against Him and demanded who should witness that Israel transgressed the Torah. God answered that the Torah herself would bear testimony to that effect. Summoned by God, the Torah appeared. Abraham reproached her, saying, "My daughter, dost thou forget how, when God did lead thee from one people to another and none would receive thee, Israel alone did welcome thee? And thou, in this nation's time of stress, wilt come up as a witness against her?" These words abashed the Torah and she refused to give evidence. Abraham was thus victorious over God. (Immanuel Olsvanger, *Contentions with God, A Study in Jewish Folklore* [Capetown, 1921], p. 8.) Olsvanger points out that according to tradition the Torah was drawn up even before the creation of the world. As Midrash says, God himself acted in accordance with it "as an architect with his plans." Olsvanger compares the Torah as the supreme law which stands above God with the Greek Tyche, to whom Zeus later eventually submitted (p. 13).

My son Arthur reminds me that I had already presented the view of the re-emerging Hebrew mother-goddess more than forty years ago in a book not yet translated (*Der Eigene und der Fremde Gott* [Vienna-Zurich, 1923], pp. 57ff.).

How could I forget that? Here is a confirmation of Freud's statement in a conversation with me that one easily forgets what one has oneself written. What one has written is, so to speak, intellectually and emotionally conquered and will therefore be easily dismissed from one's memory.

EIGHT

REMARKS ON RITUAL UNCLEANLINESS

1. Compare Max Grunwald, *Die Hygiene der Juden* (Dresden, 1911), pp. 97ff.

2. Frazer, *The Golden Bough* (abr. ed.; New York, 1958), pp. 241ff.

3. "The Canadian Déné," *Annual Archaeological Report* (Toronto, 1905), and a paper in *Anthropos*, V, 971.

4. Frazer, *op. cit.*

5. *Totem and Taboo* (New York, 1938).

6. Robert Briffault, *The Mothers* (New York, 1927), II, 665ff.

7. In his article on serpent-worship, *Encyclopedia of Religion and Ethics*, XI, 411.

8. Louis Ginzberg, *Legends of the Jews* (Philadelphia, 1938), V, 89, 106.

9. *Cultes, Myths et Religions* (Paris, 1905-12), II, 398.

10. For instance, in Robert Briffault's *The Mothers*, 397-407; in *Religion in Geschichte und Gegenwart* (3rd ed.; Tübingen, 1960); and in Ottokar Nemecek, *Virginity* (New York, 1948).

11. *Der Menstruation-Komplex* (Vienna and Leipzig, 1928).

NINE

ANCIENT LIVING RELIGION

1. A. Z. Idelsohn, *Jewish Liturgy and Its Development* (New York, 1932), p. 160.

2. *Jewish Encyclopedia*, VIII, 679.

3. *Ibid.*, IX, 244.

4. 6. Sanhedrin 42 a.

5. *Exodus and Leviticus*, p. 580.

6. *Lehrbuch der Hebräischen Archäologie* (Freiburg and Leipzig, 1894), p. 139.

7. *Prologomena zur Geschichte Israels* (2d ed.; Berlin, 1883), p. 116.

8. For instance, Hayyim Schauss, *The Jewish Festivals* (Cincinnati, 1938), pp. 274ff, and Max Joseph in *Universal Jewish Encyclopedia*, VIII, 111.

9. Schauss, *op. cit.*, 275.

10. *The Legends of the Jews* (Philadelphia, 1946), vols. I-VII.

11. *Ibid.*, I, 24.

12. *The Mothers* (New York, 1927), III, 77.

13. *Ibid.*, II, 8.

14. *Ibid.*, II, 41.

15. *Ibid.*, I, 26.

16. Samuel Ives Curtis, *Primitive Semitic Religion Today* (London, 1902), p. 106.

17. *The Five Great Monarchies*, I, 56.

18. D. Nielsen, *Die Arabische Mondreligion* (Strassburg, 1904), p. 37.

19. Maurice A. Canney, "Sun, Moon and Stars," *Encyclopedia of Religion and Ethics*, XII, 80.

20. A. Zernitz, *La Luna* (Trieste, 1889), p. 6.

21. Addendum 1963: As A. L. Sachar reports (*Sufferance Is the Badge* [New York, 1940], p. 179), the famous Rabbi Shapiro of Plotok was executed during the Polish-Russian War in 1920 on the charge that he had sent messages to the enemy. The later government investigation concluded that a terrible mistake had been made. The rabbi had been participating in the ceremony of the Blessing of the New Moon, performed outdoors by the community. The traditional rites had been interpreted by the Poles as signals to the enemy.

TEN

PRAYER SHAWLS AND PHYLACTERIES

1. Matt. 23:5.

2. Matt. 9:20.

3. Men. 42 b; Yad 111, 15.

4. Schab. 28 b.

5. Yad 11; Orach Chajim 32, 23 and 32.

6. Yad 11; 15; Orach Chajim 32, 19.

7. Rabbi Tam proposed the sequence Exod. 13:1-10; Exod. 13:11-16; Deut. 11:13-21; Deut. 6:4-9. But Raschi proposed Exod. 13:1-10; Exod. 13:11-16; Deut. 6:4-9; Deut. 11:13-21.

8. If anyone has spoken between the fixing of the hand tephillah and that of the head tephillah, he must repeat the two invocations on applying the head tephillah (Men. 36 a; Yad 1.c. IV, 4, 5.

9. Hos. 2:4, 19. One may compare with this a passage in Goethe's letter to Frau von Stein: "The Jews have thongs which they wind about their arms when they pray; so will I bind thy lovely riband about my arm when I make my prayer to thee, hoping to share in thy goodness, wisdom, moderation and patience."

10. Men. 36 b.

11. Ber. 14 b.

12. They are expressly required in Num. 15:37-40, and in Deut. 22: 11, 12. "And the Lord spake unto Moses, saying, Speak unto the children of Israel, and bid them that they make them fringes in the borders of their garments, throughout their generations, and that they put upon the fringe of the borders a riband of blue, and it shall be to you for a fringe, that ye may look upon it and remember all the commandments of the Lord and do them; and that ye seek not after your own heart and your own eyes, after which ye used to go a whoring; that ye may remember, and do all my commandments, and be holy unto your God." "Thou shalt not wear a garment of diverse sorts, as of woollen and linen together. Thou shalt make thee fringes upon the four quarters of thy vesture wherewith thou coverest thyself."

13. It may also be compared with the Greek *hymation,* a word the New Testament actually employs in its translation.

14. Jadajim III, 3.

15. Schabbath XVI, 1. See also Emil Schürer, *Geschichte des jüdischen Volkes im Zeitalter Jesu Christi* (4th ed.; Leipzig, 1907), pp. 569f.

16. Sabbath II, 3.

17. Berach I, fol. 7.

18. Isa. 17:8.

19. Deut. 33:2.

20. Ps. 29:11.

21. Deut. 32:1-3.

22. Berach I, 2.

23. Berach II, 11).

24. Psalm 26:6.

25. Berach 44, 1).

26. s. Rasch Hasch 17 a.

27. In the paraphrase to Canticle 8.

28. Jad. IV, 25, 26.

29. Menach, 43 and elsewhere.

30. Berach 30 b.

31. "Thefillin, eine Betrachtung," *Gesammelte Schriften,* II (1876), 172ff.

32. Menachoth, 43 b.

33. Sifre no. 115 to Schellach lacha, 35.

34. Sifre no. 115.

35. Schabb. 118 b.

36. Schabb. 32 b.

37. Zach. 8:23.

38. Men. 44 a.

39. (Klausenburg, 1876), p. 97.

40. "Die Totaphot nach Bibel und Tradition," *Jahrbuch für protestantische Theologie,* VII (1881), 666f.

41. Exod. 13:1-2.

42. Exod. 13:12.

43. Deut. 6:8; 11:8.

44. "Das Kainszeichen," *Zeitschr. für Alttestamentliche Wissenschaft,* XLV (1894).

45. Rev. 13:16f.; 14:9; 16:2; 19:20; 20:4.

46. Rev. 14:1.

47. Rev. 7:2ff.; 9:4.

48. Exod. 13:9.

49. Stade, *Das Kainszeichen,* p. 312.

50. Baentsch, "Exodus-Leviticus-Numeri," *Handkommentar zum Alten Testament* (1903), p. 113.

51. *Kurzer Handkommentar zum Alten Testament* (Tübingen, 1900); Exodus discussed by Holzinger.

52. *Reste arabischen Heidentums* (Berlin, 1897), p. 165.

53. "Divination and Magic in Deut. 17:10 and 11," *The Journal of Philology,* XIII (1885), 286.

54. Max Grünbaum, *Ges Aufsätze zur Sprach-und Sagenkunde* (Berlin, 1901), pp. 208f.

55. Ludwig Blau, *Das altjüdische Zauberwesen* (Strassburg, 1898), pp. 87f.

56. Wilhelm Bousset, *Die Religion des Judentums im späthellenischen Zeitlater* (3rd ed.; Tübingen, 1926), p. 179.

57. Emil Schürer, *Geschichte des jüdischen Volkes im Zeitalter Jesu Christi,* II (4th ed.; Leipzig, 1907), p. 568.

58. *Realenzyklopädie für protestantische Theologie,* V, 693.

59. *Geschichte des Volkes Israel,* II (4th ed.; Gotha, 1922), p. 76.

60. *Hebräische Archäologie.*

61. Friedländer, *Der Antichrist in den vorchristlichen Quellen* (Göttingen, 1901), pp. 161f.

62. *Ibid.,* p. 157.

63. "Phylacteries," *The Jewish Encyclopedia,* X, 26.

64. "Phylacteries," *The International Standard Bible Encyclopedia,* IV.

65. "Phylacteries," *A Dictionary of the Bible*, III, pp. 871f.

66. Exod. 18:16; Deut. 6:8; 11:8.

67. Kennedy, in *A Dictionary of the Bible*, p. 871.

68. "Tephillin," Herzog's *Realenzyklopädie für protestantische Theologie*, XIV, 512.

69. "Die Totaphot nach Bibel und Tradition," *Jahrbuch für protestantische Theologie*, VII (1881), 678.

70. "Gebet im Alten Testament," Herzog's *Realenzyklopädie für protestantische Theologie*, VI, 393.

71. Kennedy, in *A Dictionary of the Bible*, p. 872.

72. E. Kautzsch, ed., *Die Apokryphen und Pseudoepigraphen des Alten Testamentes*, II, 19; Aristeas' letter of 159 B.C. (in Wendland's translation) states: "And he expressly commanded that the commemoration signs should be applied likewise on the hands." Cf. also Hodey, "Aristae Historia," in *De Bibliorum Textibus*, p. 18.

73. A critical examination soon exposes the weakness of this argument. Kennedy's choice of a date is based upon aphoristic expressions and their period. He assumes without question that he is dealing with a metaphorical mode of expression, and so arrives at a definite date. But it is extremely doubtful whether these verses of the Bible are of a metaphorical character. What he alleges in favor of the Pharisees, as a psychological probability, is somewhat superficial, and one has the impression that his judgment is unconsciously influenced by the recollection of Christ's protest. That the tephillin were worn at this time does not prove that they were not worn long before this period.

74. Ant. IV, VIII.

75. Rodkinsohn, *Ursprung und Entwicklung des Phylakterienritus bei den Juden* (1883). See review in the *Revue des Études Juives*, VI, 288.

76. *Rituels* Accad., 57n. 95.

77. Wilkinson, *Ancient Egyptians* (London, 1854), Plate II b.

78. Exod. 28:33; 29:25.

79. As a survival which, like the fantastic animals in our churches, served to intimidate the demons and evil spirits. *The Book of Exodus* (1908), p. 185.

80. *Lectures on the Religions of the Semites* (1889), p. 334.

81. In the Vulgate Latin version of the Bible: *Et erit quasi signum in manu tua et quasi monumentum ante oculos tuos.* . . .

82. Baentsch, "Exodus-Leviticus-Numeri," *Handkommentar zum Alten Testament* (1903), p. 111.

83. Holzinger, *Exodus* (Tübingen, 1900), p. 41.

84. *A Dictionary of the Bible,* III, 871.

85. Alfred Bertholet, "Deuteronomium," in *Kurzer Handkommentar zum Alten Testament* (Freiburg, 1899), p. 23.

86. *Ibid.* (2d ed., 1923).

87. Kennedy, *loc. cit.,* p. 871.

88. "The Ancient Jewish Sanctuaries/ Divine Service and Customs/ Made Plain/ in an Exhaustive Description of the Entire Levite Priesthood/ And Five Separate Books, etc."

89. *Ibid.,* p. 800.

90. *Ibid.,* p. 802.

91. J. G. Frazer, *Totemism and Exogamy,* I, 26ff.

92. Lewis and Clarke, *Journey to the Source of the Missouri River,* I, 123. Cited from Frazer.

93. W. Robertson Smith, *Lectures on the Religions of the Semites* (3rd ed.; London, 1927), pp. 436ff.

94. A discussion of the problem of which was the original totemic animal of the Israelites will be found in my book *Das Ritual* (2d ed.; Vienna, 1928).

95. *Loc. cit.,* p. 798.

96. Cf. Hermann J. Wurm, *Die Papstwahl* (Cologne, 1902), p. 94.

97. No one familiar with the subject will harbor any doubt as to the connection between these two religious objects, though to the best of my knowledge no one has hitherto elucidated the connection.

The scapular consists of two scraps of woollen cloth which are so connected by two strings that one of the pieces of cloth lies on the chest and the other between the shoulders. "The material of the scapular must be wool, not cotton, linen, or silk, and a woven woollen fabric is required, not knitted or otherwise prepared. As regards the shape, the scapular must consist of two square pieces of woollen cloth. When the sacred Congregation was asked whether round or oval or polygonal scapulars can be effectively consecrated, the answer was: *Nihil esse innovandum.*" (Beringer, *Die Ablässe, ihr Wesen und Gebrauch* [10th ed.; Paderborn, 1893], pp. 557ff.).

Not only the form and function, but also the particular features of the scapular recall the corresponding features of the tallith. The scapular must always be worn, day and night. If one were to go a whole day without wearing the scapular, one would not be able to obtain indulgences for that day. Also, it must be worn in a certain manner, so that one of the woollen strips hangs over the breast, etc. The further development of the ritual of the scapular became more and more complicated as the number of scapulars increased. Thus, the red scapular of the Passion was introduced by Pius IX in 1847 and provided with special indulgences, on account of an apparition which the Saviour vouchsafed to a Sister of Mercy. The blue scapular of the Immaculate Conception was revealed in the seventeenth century to the Venerable Ursula Berincasa in Naples, while the Heart of Jesus scapular is attributed to Maria Alacoque. Beringer (p. 374) asserts that devotion to the Lord Jesus scapular has greatly increased, "since in the war of 1870 its miraculous effects were noted in the case of many soldiers." Devotion to the brown Carmelite scapular, the most widespread of all, is due to a famous apparition of the Mother of God, which was vouchsafed on Sunday, July 16, 1251, at Cambridge to the holy Simon Stock, the general of the Carmelites. The Holy Virgin addressed the saint, showing him a scapular, and saying: "Whosoever dies with this upon him will not suffer the eternal fire." The Virgin, however, vouchsafed yet a further privilege to those who devoutly wear the scapular of the Carmelites. This assurance was communciated to Pope John XXII, to whom the Virgin appeared, promising him to liberate the wearers of this scapular from Purgatory as quickly as possible, and explicitly on the Saturday after their decease. The Pope announced this grace, the so-called Privilegium Sabbatinum, in the Bull of March 5, 1330. Benedict XIV undertook to defend this privilege against its presumptuous critics. Many popes, among them Clement VII, Paul III, Pius V, and Gregory XIII, have declared themselves enthusiastic supporters of this privilege. By the decree of the Congregation of April 27, 1887 it was decided that with regard to the special reverance and devotion pertaining to this most ancient scapular, it shall not be worn with other scapulars, but shall be consecrated and worn separately.

98. Cf. Georg Beer, *Pascha* (Tübingen, 1911), pp. 18ff.; and N. M. Nicolsky, "Pascha im Kulte des jerusalemischen Tempels" in *Zeitschr. für altest. Wiss.*, III (1927).

99. The Passah sacrifice now consisted of sheep and goats (Exod. 12:1) and of sheep and oxen (Deut. 16:2). One may assume that originally the bull was the Passah or paschal animal.

100. The circling round the sacrificial animal is followed later by the circling round the altar. This constitutes the most important part of divine worship among the ancient Arabians (cf. Wellhausen, Skizzen, III 2, p. 109; *Heiler*, Gebet 2, pp. 101, 103). For the Old Testament, cf. I Kings 18:26; Psalm 42:5; 118, 27ff.

101. "Der Versöhnungstag," *Imago*, VI (1920).

102. "Das jüdische Speiseritual," *Imago*, XIII, Parts 2-4. This appreciation of my predecessors, whose analytic conclusions agree in essentials with those developed in these pages, does not mean that I share their opinions in every detail. For instance, the explanation of the origin of the head tephillah in Fromm-Reichmann's treatise appears to me extremely improbable. The authoress holds that we are dealing with the result of "a simple displacement mechanism," "when the second cube, that is, the second horn is removed from the forehead to the upper arm." In my opinion, this displacement mechanism is neither so simple nor so obvious as she supposes.

Presumably we have an artificial substitute for the hoof of the animal, which was originally represented quite realistically on the hand, but which was subsequently, under the combined influences of various motives, among which the tendency toward disguise was especially prominent, was moved higher up the arm. For the rest, we have now seen by what obscure byways the orthodox tradition of the Judaic law returns to indicate the original significance of a cultic detail. When many pious Jews, in order to overcome the uncertainty arising from the discussion between Rabbi Raschi and Rabbi Tamm, decide to wear two head tephillin, we may readily recognize, in this distorted form, the ancient sign of the paired horns, the return of the repressed.

103. Addendum 1963: While on the parchment scroll of the phylacteries put on daily by the Jews is written "Hear, O Israel," on the phylacteries God puts on are written the words "Who is like unto thy people Israel, only nation on the earth" (Sanhedrin 7, 14).

At a certain period there were in the Soviet Union such slogans as: "Sell your prayer shawls for the benefit of the industrialization" or "Convert your phylacteries into tractors!" (Abraham Leon Sachar, *Sufferance Is the Badge* [New York, 1939], p. 162).

In Jerusalem is a Chamber of Martyrs in which the bayonet-slashed prayer shawls of Orthodox Jews murdered by the Nazis are shown.

ELEVEN

THE SIGN LANGUAGE OF PRIESTLY BLESSING

1. In my book *Das Ritual* (Vienna, 1919; English edition, London, 1931; American edition, 1946).

2. "Der Versöhnungstag," *Imago*, VI (1920). English translation in Karl Abraham's *Selected Papers* (London, 1955).

3. *Der jüdische Gottesdienst* (Leipzig, 1931), p. 68.

4. Quoted by Ismar Elbogen in "Priestly Blessing" in *Universal Jewish Encyclopedia*, VIII, 634.

5. "The Day of Atonement" in *Selected Papers*, p. 145.

6. Compare Part Ten.

7. Compare the chapter "God's Incorporeality" in this writer's *Mystery on the Mountain* (New York, 1959), pp. 159ff.

TWELVE

FAMILY SOLIDARITY

1. *Family Behavior* (New York, 1936), p. 273.

2. *Harper's Magazine*, September 1931.

3. To cite only a few: Ernest Jones (*Free Associations, Memories of a Psychoanalyst* [New York, 1959], p. 209) speaks of the Jewish family

atmosphere, with its intensities and frictions which he considers "somewhat trying but one could be sure of never being bored." Karl Menninger (*A Psychiatric World* [New York, 1937]) comments on the "very frequently observed tendency among Jews in their overemphasis of the family bond and their overprotection and over-demonstrativeness toward the children." Harold D. Lasswell says in his contribution to *The Jew in a Gentile World* (edited by Arnold A. Rogow [New York, 1961], p. 373): "In the sphere of friendship and intimacy Jews have been loved for lively warmth of personality and family devotion." George A. Barton (in his article on the Semites, *Encyclopedia of Ancient Religion and Ethics,* XI, 382) points to the Arab jubilant at the birth of a son and refers to the "delight in offspring and devotion to family that is characteristic of the Jews to this day."

4. Yet Peah I, 15d.

5. *Jewish Life in the Middle Ages* (London, 1896), p. 113.

6. Quoted in *Encyclopedia of Religion and Ethics,* V, 741.

7. *Jewish Family Solidarity* (Vicksburg, 1940), p. 17.

8. *Ibid.,* p. 65.

9. *Ibid.,* p. 71.

10. *Letters of Sigmund Freud* (New York, 1960), p. 302.

11. *The Rothschilds* (New York, 1962), p. 15.

12. *Ibid.,* p. 29.

13. *Ibid.,* p. 219.

14. *Ibid.,* p. 174.

15. *Encyclopedia of Religion and Ethics,* V, 742.

16. Nicolas Hobbs, "Sources of Gain in Psychotherapy," *American Psychologist,* November 1962, p. 741.

17. Ernst Elster (ed.), *Sämtliche Werke,* VI, 453.

18. A leading British historian, C. V. Wedgewood, deals with this subject in her book *Truth and Opinion* (London, 1960). She remarks: "The careful, thorough and accurate answer to the question *How?*

should take the historian a long way towards answering the question *Why?* . . . ."

19. The tribe *"naît soit du dévelopement d'un clan, soit de la fusion entre clans différents."* Louis-Germain Lévy, *La Famille dans l'antiquité Israélite* (Paris, 1904), p. 71.

20. *Israel* (Copenhagen, 1926), pp. 46ff.

21. *Ibid.*, p. 48.

22. *Ibid.*, p. 49.

23. *Ibid.*, p. 495.

24. *Ibid.*, p. 496.

25. Quoted from the Meridian Library edition, p. 277.

26. Addendum 1963: In his psychoanalytic study *Christians and Jews* (New York, 1951), p. 120, Rudolph M. Lowenstein points out that Jewish solidarity, "although greatly exaggerated by the Gentiles," exists in the religious fellowship in times of persecution. The French writer Charles Peguy gives a vivid example of that reaction through identification in his portrait of Bernard Lazare: "Here was a man who would snatch up a newspaper and skimming rapidly through its four, six or eight pages, would pounce on one line, and in that line would be the word 'Jew.' Here was a man, a seasoned newspaperman, mind you, who would grow red or turn pale at some chance phrase in a newspaper—some excerpt from an article, some cable or by-line—if this chance phrase, this cable or by-line contained the word 'Jew.' He had a heart that bled in every ghetto in the world: a heart that bled in Roumania and Turkey, in Russia and the Argentine, in America and Hungary; in short wherever Jews are persecuted, which is as much as to say everywhere. Such is your Jew aquiver with rage. A creature in a state of perpetual tension, bearing the weight of a whole race, a whole world on his shoulders—fifty centuries of history on his bowed shoulders."

Lowenstein considers this common awareness of past, present and possible future suffering as "one of the strongest bonds uniting the Jews of the world" (page 121).

Let me add here an old Jewish saying: *Parents would break the skies into pieces in order to educate their sons.*

EPILOGUE

1. Addendum 1963: The Austrian writer Richard Flatter had translated *King Lear* into German and Freud had thanked him for sending him this work. In his letter of March 30, 1930 (now to be found in *The Life and Work of Sigmund Freud* by Ernest Jones, III, 452), Freud also discussed the question whether one is justified in considering Lear a case of hysteria. Freud did not think one should expect from a poet a clinically correct description of an emotional disturbance, but points out that Lear's normal behavior when he knows he is safely protected by Cordelia does not justify a diagnosis of hysteria. (Flatter's translation is now available in his *Shakespeare, neu übersetzt* [Vienna and Zurich, 1952].)

2. Jones, *op.* cit., p. 457.

INDEX